THE
VIP
PRINCIPLE

THE
VIP
PRINCIPLE

Discover How Guest Experiences
Drive Long Term Growth

LESSONS FROM
THE GAMING AND
CASINO INDUSTRY

MICHELLE PASCOE AND DAVE STAUGHTON
♥   ♠   ♦   ♣

Published by Advantage, Charleston, South Carolina.
Member of Advantage Media Group.

ADVANTAGE is a registered trademark and the Advantage colophon is a trademark of Advantage Media Group, Inc.

Printed in the United States of America.

ISBN: 978-1-59932-557-6
LCCN: 2015940224

Book design by Megan Elger.

This publication is designed to provide accurate and authoritative information in regard to the subject matter covered. It is sold with the understanding that the publisher is not engaged in rendering legal, accounting, or other professional services. If legal advice or other expert assistance is required, the services of a competent professional person should be sought.

Advantage Media Group is proud to be a part of the Tree Neutral® program. Tree Neutral offsets the number of trees consumed in the production and printing of this book by taking proactive steps such as planting trees in direct proportion to the number of trees used to print books. To learn more about Tree Neutral, please visit www.treeneutral.com. To learn more about Advantage's commitment to being a responsible steward of the environment, please visit www.advantagefamily.com/green

Advantage Media Group is a publisher of business, self-improvement, and professional development books and online learning. We help entrepreneurs, business leaders, and professionals share their Stories, Passion, and Knowledge to help others Learn & Grow. Do you have a manuscript or book idea that you would like us to consider for publishing? Please visit advantagefamily.com or call 1.866.775.1696.

MICHELLE PASCOE, MANAGING DIRECTOR, OPTIMUM OPERATING PROCEDURES AND SERVICES, PTY., LTD.

Michelle Pascoe lives and breathes her passion for Customer Service, Mystery Shopping, and Team Motivation. She is an experienced businesswoman and specialist in every aspect of service operations and processes and their impact on the customer experience.

In 1994 she founded one of Australia's most respected training and research companies, Optimum Operating Procedures and Services Pty., Ltd. (OOPS). Now a thriving provider of Mystery Shopping, Service Benchmarking, Surveys and Focus Groups, Competitor Audits, Team Training and Manager Leadership Development, Michelle has applied the very tips and techniques that she presents to achieving her own business success.

As an International Certified Speaking Professional and Accredited Trainer and Assessor, Michelle combines her extensive experience and specialised knowledge with an absolute commitment to igniting the potential in each and every individual so her clients can achieve outstanding results. Her programme participants—from across the gaming industry, hospitality, retail, manufacturing, real estate, government, automotive and professional services sectors—walk away from her presentations feeling inspired, educated and equipped to deliver outstanding service experiences.

Employing a team of more than sixty, working with multimillion-dollar clients and coaching the leaders of tomorrow as well as small and medium-size enterprise (SME) entrepreneurs, Michelle believes in seeing and igniting the potential in everyone.

Her key focus and passion pertains to service delivery and the expectations of the twenty-first-century customer, through mapping the journey of today's customer, and she believes that no matter the industry, service is the key point of difference in creating the essential human connection. Today's customer is more connected, competitive, optimistic and relentless in their pursuit of value, driving the changes in how businesses (even large corporations) deliver their product or service.

DAVID STAUGHTON, BSc (HONS), AFAIM, CCEO, MIMC

Dave Staughton is a scientist, author and award-winning businessman who helps businesses find more opportunities to make sales all year round. An expert on business development and cross-selling in a transforming marketplace, Dave can show you how to make the most of everything you already have.

Dave has over thirty years' experience in a broad range of industries, including mining, retail, hospitality and consulting. He's been passionate about business since starting work in the family-owned hardware store at age 6.

Dave worked for five of Australia's largest mining companies and then started his own business. He became a millionaire by age 30. In fifteen years, he grew a multi-business hospitality empire in Melbourne, Australia, before joining a fast-growing consulting practice specialising in growing businesses. With an expertise in making off-peak sales and filling quiet times, he has been instrumental in numerous multimillion-dollar sales turnarounds. Dave is a keen advocate and practitioner of the three Rs of business: repeats, referrals and reputation building.

Dave has worked with hotels, gaming venues, pubs, clubs, restaurants, bars, function and event venues, hotels, motels, RV parks, ferries, bus lines, trains and even airlines to boost their brands and build their business. Dave's consulting and training clients include multinationals, nationally listed companies and groups of small businesses seeking to radically lift team member engagement levels and boost sales results.

Dave is an energising and entertaining speaker and has been performing in front of an audience for over twenty years. A walking library of business case studies, funny quotes and real-life experiences, he inspires people with his passion, energy and enthusiasm.

PREFACE

Whether you are looking to expand an already successful business or revamp one that's not living up to expectations, this book will walk you through what it takes to bring your venue up to the next level by retaining and creating VIP guests.

Written by two leading experts in Guest Service and Sales, this book draws on their 50+ years of combined knowledge of and experience in the hospitality industry to map the VIP Journey of your guests. Don't be surprised if you find your own company and employees in this book, reflected in real case studies and scenarios. While this book is aimed primarily at the broader hospitality industry—Casinos, Resorts, Clubs, Hotels, Restaurants, Entertainment and Conference Centres—the VIP Journey can be incorporated into any industry that wants to offer more to its clients by understanding their needs and consistently surpassing them.

THE VIP JOURNEY
The essentials of creating a VIP culture
- Approaching continuous improvement step by step—no magic wands!
- Regular in-depth measurement of guest experience
- Unrelenting focus on your guests' needs and wants

- Developing leaders, teamwork and multi-skilling
- Creating a workplace of choice—values and ethics
- Analysing results—a commitment to taking action
- Gathering competitor intelligence and creating customised guest offers
- Celebrating success—"we" not "me"

STARTING OUT ON THE V.I.P. JOURNEY

CASE STUDY: VIP VENUE IMPROVEMENT JOURNEY

Since the 1990s, we have worked with management and front-line teams at some of the largest venues in the gaming industry in Sydney, Australia. One such long-term and highly successful client has expanded its footprint to seven satellite sites and is considered to be one of the biggest gaming venue groups in Australia. We have tracked its journey since 1999 with qualitative and quantitative research: Mystery Shopping, Guest Surveys and Focus Groups, going beyond the "yes and no" of service. Our team works collaboratively with venue managers, developing our proprietary reporting programme to fulfil their needs and continually improve their business.

Successful hospitality businesses are always looking for new ways to attract and retain their equivalent of the casino industry's High Roller, that free-spending frequent guest who's both the most sought after and the most fickle. The twenty-first-century guest is seeking an "experience", not just a transaction. Being Australian, we call it the Tim Tam® moment, because of the beloved Arnott's Tim Tam®, a favourite chocolate treat to many around the world that goes beyond the biscuit lover's expectations, every mouthful, every time. It is all about differentiating your destination by adding value to what you are offering and giving your guests the WOW factor. Join us as we Map the Journey from "so-so" to "so amazing!" for your business, whether you are a smaller venue or a sprawling destination. It is about the choices we make as individuals and a team.

But first, let's take a trip through some of the ways it can go terribly wrong ...

WELCOME TO HOTEL APATHY—THROUGH THE EYES OF A MYSTERY SHOPPER

After a long week at work, you look forward to a weekend away to relax, to enjoy a good meal and entertainment. You have been reading through the social media hangouts about where to go and where not to go, thanks to the ever-busy twenty-first-century guests who like to connect everyone to their meals and experiences. You have asked around, reviewed websites, made a decision and booked online. Your expectations are high; it is going to be an amazing weekend.

The journey begins as you drive around the multi-level car park, finally squeezing into a space that would be more suitable for a motor scooter, so your partner has to get out before you park—but, hey, it is the only space available. As you push upon the heavy glass door leading into the foyer, you are in awe of the surroundings. You can smell and feel the luxury, fine cuisine and the air of anticipation. Then your eyes lock with the cold, steely eyes of the security guard—you think—until you get closer and read his badge: "Guest Relations Officer". He juts his chin forward in an upward direction, which means, "Good evening! Welcome. Do you have any ID? We hope you have a wonderful night." At least that's what you assume it means, because all he does is examine your ID, grunt and thrust it back at you.

The venue is strikingly decorated with lounges, plants and lighting placed strategically to encourage the feeling of warmth and welcome. Too bad the staff isn't nearly as inviting. As you move to the bar, the loud thumping music surrounds you as you become just another unimpressed guest in an ever-growing crowd. Something is not right; there isn't much chatter or laughter. Then you hear it: the smashing of bottles into a steel bin by the bar person who, instead of walking to the bin, likes to show off his baseball skills by pitching the empties from the bar. The stench of wet bar mats rises to your nose as the puddles on the bar top stain the sleeve of your new white shirt. What little ambience there was has now been shattered like an empty bottle, so you and your partner decide to move on to dinner.

The dining room is empty, but the host still asks if you have a booking and spends the next minute brooding over the bookings diary while carrying on a whispered conversation with their dining room counterpart. You weave amongst the chairs much like a maze and are shown to the closest table to the restroom, with one chair jammed up against the wall. Grateful that you went on that diet, you slide in, banging your knee against the leg of the table that now has a distinct wobble every time you put the slightest pressure on it, since you dislodged the wedge of paper from under the leg.

You place your order and wait patiently for forty-five minutes until you catch the eye of the waiter by standing and waving at them. They haven't been back since they delivered the table water. They look at you quizzically and go to the kitchen, eventually returning after serving other tables, to inform you that your order had been lost but it will only be another five minutes, which, of course, turns into twenty.

With no offer of dessert or coffee at the completion of your main course, and although you are still hungry and thirsty thanks to the meagre portions, inedible gristly steak, and no drinks except for the warm table water, you ask for the bill, only to be told that you have to go to the register to pay.

After leaving the restaurant, you wander off to see the entertainment in the lounge, hoping it will save the evening. The singer isn't too bad when the microphone isn't squealing with feedback. However, the lights are very high and positioned so that you are bathed in a white light that is making you see spots, and you spill your drink.

You move to the gaming floor and as you sit at the gaming machine, you press the drinks button, and after five minutes, you are approached by a gum-chewing team member who obviously doesn't enjoy their job. After pushing past you to turn off the button, they bark, "What can I get you?" After a while, the team member returns with a plastic cup of a lukewarm, flat beverage that may once have contained ice cubes a few hours ago. Observing the guest next to you picking the best out of the box of assorted hot snacks she has ordered, you decide to skip that treat.

Upon leaving the venue, you receive no farewell, as the team members are having a wonderful time sharing stories of their big weekend and passing judgement on what guests are wearing and if they looked in the mirror when they left home!

You head for the lift lobby and wait patiently, as only two lifts out of five are working. As you alight from the lift, you recoil from the odour of stale egg and ketchup that is congealed on the plates piled high on trays outside rooms. You don't have far to go, as the room is beside the lift, and after you manage to get the access card working upon the fifth attempt, you enter your room.

The air conditioning sounds like an Airbus taking off but produces no discernible cooling. The pillows may as well be sacks of sand. Looking out the window, you discover you have a view … of garbage bins, not the water view that was promised when you made the online booking, and your phone charger cord won't reach the power outlet behind the bedhead, so you begin to move the furniture.

The next day, after being awoken by the shrill sound of the bedside alarm clock, set by a previous guest, you go downstairs to check out. At the counter you are asked, "Did you enjoy your stay?" The team member continues to smile but doesn't offer any apology when you list the complaints. The team member just hands you the paperwork and says, "Thank you. Next, please."

Thank you, Hotel Apathy. We won't be back and neither will our hundreds of social media contacts and their friends. It won't be a "ripple"; it will be a tidal wave.

The evaluation: "Never again!"

Of course, this example is extreme. However, at some point, we have seen or experienced *all* of these examples of poor service and disappointing facilities that add up to an awful experience we will never forget—or forgive.

Having a magnificent venue is one thing, but it's the human factor that makes the difference. Over the years, we have heard too many times from senior management that a human resources/employee relations department costs money. That is a totally wrong assumption. If you are not hiring the right people, training and nurturing them in their roles, and performance-managing those who are not the right fit, your business will not succeed to its full potential, as you will always be trying to fix the leaks.

Success in the hospitality business is first and foremost about service and a great guest experience. This book looks at the VIP Principle: the Venue Improvement Journey. It is a proven methodology, based on our research and experience, and it will lead you and your team on the journey to success.

CONTENTS

CHAPTER 1

Starting Out On The VIP Journey

Find Out Where You Are With Mapping, Measuring And Focus Groups

Mantra: Start where you are. Find out what you have. Map your VIP Journey.

In navigating today's fast-moving hospitality industry, ignorance is something you can't afford. Things have changed: your guests have higher expectations than ever before, and in learning to draw and keep twenty-first-century guests, you need to know how they see and engage in your venue. If you are not in the business of listening to them, you may not be in business for long.

Why should you measure what you do? More than ever, you are dealing with a diverse public and workforce: multiple generations, cultures, languages and expectations. Great service is the benchmark today; getting that service out of your team on a regular basis is the goal. Identifying where you are succeeding and where you are failing is the big first step to raising your operating standards. Given the increasing competition for the guests' dollar, the stakes have never been higher. And you'd better believe that your competitors already have their own journey maps.

THERE ARE SIX KEY MEASURING TOOLS TO ASSESS AND ANALYSE YOUR GUEST OFFERING:

1. Mystery Shopping

2. Focus Groups

3. Online Forums

4. Benchmarking

5. Trends Analysis

6. Competitor Audit/Positioning Map

Using this research, we can map your position and help guide you to higher ground, using a suite of customised proprietary reports. The real value is in knowing how to read the results and presenting them in a way that lets you see where your venue is both succeeding and coming up short.

WHAT YOU SEE DEPENDS ON YOUR POINT OF VIEW ...

Everybody involved in your venue has a different view of the business: there are the views of the manager, the front-line team, guests and even an independent consultant's view. Through mapping, measuring and collecting feedback, we can tell you how your venue appears through the eyes of your guests—and how your front-line team provides service to interact and engage with them.

Managers look down and into the business. The team members look out, because they are looking after your guests. The stakeholders are looking at the bottom line, so they are thinking in terms of the future and the necessary strategic planning to get there. As consultants, we are tasked with figuring out how you can keep bringing that essential "WOW" factor to your guests every day, both now and into the future.

MAPPING THE JOURNEY—WITH RESEARCH YOU CAN

- Know your competitors

- Expand your service offering

- Become a "one-stop shop" that offers a wide array of facilities

- Create a successful loyalty programme

- Renovate and rebuild

- Grow by amalgamation

- Build a business empire

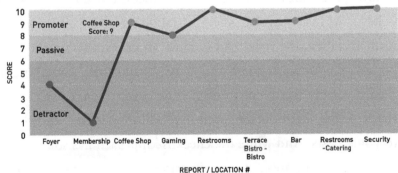

THE SIX ESSENTIAL RESEARCH TOOLS FOR MAPPING THE VIP JOURNEY

With over two decades of experience, we have developed and used these customised research tools to provide the best analysis.

1. **Mystery Shopping:** Whether it is undertaken face to face, online or over the telephone, Mystery Shopping provides a true view of the guest experience of your service and/or product. Depending on the depth of information your venue requires and the end goal for this information, the report that each Mystery Shopper completes could be a simple "tick and flick" done in less than ten questions, a report that is written as a "story" of the experience or a more comprehensive report that offers both qualitative and quantitative research and analysis, looking at all departments and facilities, supported by trends analysis and benchmarking over varying periods of time.

At its beginnings, Mystery Shopping was more about making lists and checking to see that team members followed those lists: If there were ten steps to putting together a hamburger, did the team member follow them exactly so that all the ingredients were on the bun, and did they remember to upsize the customer's order?

The model of using a checklist to see that your team uniformly follows procedures is still part of the process but only a part. We believe, for instance, that relevant training goes beyond teaching team members the *what* and is more about explaining the *why*, because if your team doesn't know why you expect something of them, they are likely not to do it. Remember Gen Y is all about the *why*. Tell them the *why*, and they will impart that knowledge to your guests. And while the checklist approach has some value, it doesn't, for instance, cover a situation in which the system itself has broken down and the team member has had to step up. What if you, as a loyal guest, are waiting in line to become a member, but when you get to the window, the card-reading machine has broken down? That would look bad in a simple statistical chart, but if the team member handled it creatively, turning a potentially negative experience into a positive one, that needs to be reflected, too.

It is no longer just a matter of ticking off ten questions; to accurately measure how a venue is serving its guests, you have to be ready to look at every working part, from the restroom hand driers to the placement and design of the gaming machines, dining choices and other facilities. Without that information, you are not really measuring what matters.

For team members to do their jobs well, they have to know their venue's procedures as well as the expectations of management and guests. The guest is "king" and clearly the key to improved organisational performance. A happy guest is critical to a happy environment; this is the key to repeat business and is important as an advocate in the insatiable quest for new guests.

But all Mystery Shoppers aren't created equal, nor are all surveys. One company we know sent underqualified team members out to a venue, where they simply walked around and interviewed all those they could find willing talk to them, who turned out to be the people waiting in line to use the restroom. Not surprisingly, the result was that 97% of the people surveyed said that the venue needed more toilets!

That's what Mystery Shopping has over normal member surveys. If you are only interviewing people in the foyer, the gaming room, or the bar, you will only get answers that reflect those peoples' interests in that specific area. But with Mystery Shopping, you are getting the real guest experience, because your shoppers are putting themselves into that role. It matters, too, that the "shopper" is well qualified. When selecting a Mystery Shopper, make sure that the person is trained to accurately rate what they are seeing and understand what the client is looking for. Every report should be tailored with specific questions providing valuable information to management in pursuit of improved guest service.

Good Mystery Shoppers are primed with questions designed to provide exactly the feedback the client needs—and this is done on a regular basis. Do the team members smile if guests happen to catch their eye? Do they ask your guests' how their day has been? Do they notice that a guest's coffee cup is empty, and instead of just picking it up and walking off, come over to the guest and say, "Oh, did you enjoy that coffee?" and offer a little chitchat? Do they offer to bring the guest another coffee? This kind of service is what creates the WOW experience the guest wants. Another important key is knowing the guests' names. "Sir" or "ma'am" are fine, but what if team members greet guests by their name? How much more special will that make guests feel? Training your team to do these things is what creates the connection and then conducting mystery shopping to ensure the front-line team are putting the training into practice every day with every interaction and the management team are cohesive and working toward the common goals.

Here are three popular Mystery Shopping report styles that we offer:

1. Business Insight report

2. Venue Evaluation report

3. Mapping the Guest Journey report

2. **Focus Groups**: These used to mean having a group of participants sit around a table, answering questions while the business owner or other stakeholders sat behind a one-way mirror, observing. That's changed: today, stakeholders are in the room, listening and asking questions. Another piece of this new focus group involves creating forums online weeks before the focus group is conducted in order to connect and build relationships with the participants. Quality is better than quantity: having four participants who have strong viewpoints and are articulate about them is more valuable than having twenty less-invested participants in the room, with the moderator trying to control the outspoken and coax answers from those who are only there for the financial incentive and clearly don't use the product or service.

Online forums are a useful tool for engaging guests. We have found that some people are more comfortable sharing their thoughts online than they might be in a group, especially when cultural beliefs or personality types might make it awkward for them to answer some questions face to face. Additionally, in order to participate, they have to be willing to share a photo of themselves (face blurred) in their home, providing greater insights into their day-to-day lives.

Online forums have to be engaging and conducted on a social media channel where your desired demographic participates. The key is to have a good moderator who asks the right questions to make all participants comfortable and secure in sharing their answers in an online community. There have been highly successful online forums allowing people to voice their point of view and provide feedback on products and services.

STATS

Nothing works better than asking people what they want and then giving it to them (within reason). It is all about taking the time to sit down and listen, not just listen to your gaming players but also listen to your best dining and bar guests. A range of generations including Gen Y/Z/millennials are your future; they spend most of their time playing on their mobile devices. What can you offer them to bring them into your venue and change their game-playing strategy?

3. **Benchmarking:** Industry benchmarking offers you the chance to see how your venue measures up—and not only in your region—against others that set the gold standard for the industry; your

target or benchmark should be raised on a regular basis, because if you are not constantly striving to improve, you are going to slip back. It means tweaking what you have got. It is making every team member responsible and accountable for everything they say, everything they do for your guests. It is also about having management there not just to supervise them but also to guide them and give them the resources they need. If your venue attains our industry OOPS benchmark of 96% or above, that's the WOW factor. Your venue has gone above and beyond.

4. **Trends Analysis:** Tracking trends over a period of time, whether it be three months or a year or more, provides an overview. A customised online reporting system can provide you with information on your venue's score against an industry standard (industry average). A Trends Analysis report will provide you specific information for each area of your venue, with graphic and statistical data showing the deficiencies and strengths, supported by suggestions/solutions to address the deficiencies and enhance the strengths.

5. **Competitor Audit/Positioning Map:** A Comparative Analysis programme is perfect for venues that are facing new competitors or the refurbishment of a venue in their catchment area. It is also ideal for venues that are considering a new acquisition or are about to embark on a major marketing campaign. This information can also be easily exported into other documents such as marketing plans, strategic plans or board papers.

If you are considering an expansion of your venue or taking over an existing site, start by mapping out the competition in the local area—hotels, clubs, fine dining restaurants—anything that could attract clients away from your venue. Then undertake a Mystery Shopping Competitor Audit to examine each venue's food selection, pricing, opening and closing times, promotions, websites and social media. This audit will clearly identify your target demographic and what sets you apart from your competition.

DRAGON TIP

If you are looking to attract an Asian clientele, don't forget that Feng Shui plays a big part in those cultures—and the Feng Shui of your establishment, as it is located, laid out and designed, speaks volumes to them about how lucky (or not!) they will be there. If this demographic is a big part of your clientele, you will find it worthwhile to consult a Feng Shui expert in how to make your venue even more inviting.

MEASURING THE EFFECTIVENESS OF SIGNAGE AND TEAM INTERACTION

If you are serving a largely Asian clientele, your Mystery Shoppers need to come from those cultures, too. The Chinese, for instance, are looking for luxury, so the décor has to be amazing. In many venues, you don't get the WOW factor until you walk in the door, whereas in Macau or Las Vegas, a lot of that WOW factor is outside. That WOW factor can backfire if you happen to offend the rules of Feng Shui, however. Some things you might think of as decorative could actually be seen as unlucky.

Your food offerings, too, should reflect the tastes of these guests, which means that in addition to the usual things, you need to make sure that the Chinese restaurant on your premises offers a genuine Chinese menu rather than a westernised one. Do you have team members who are multilingual and identified with a name tag bearing a national flag to symbolise the language they speak? Are you acknowledging their preferences for lots of gold in the décor? That ties in with their sense that your place is lucky. If you are not paying attention to cultural diversity in your venue, seeing your service and offerings through their eyes, you are missing out.

Using the Six Key Measuring Tools to Map your VIP Journey provides a clearer understanding of:

- Guest experience

- Employee engagement

- Employee knowledge

- Image: personal and premises

- Marketing and promotions

- Team training required

- Facilities to be added or enhanced

- Cultural diversity and opportunities

CHAPTER 2

The VIP Principle

Focus On Your Current And Identify Your Prospective VIP Guests

Mantra: Where your attention goes, money flows.

WHO IS A VIP GUEST?

The first step on the VIP Journey is to focus on identifying your ideal guests. Let's define a VIP as a Very Important Patron or Very Important Player. VIPs are those guests who are most important to the ongoing success of your venue. Typically, they can be high-spending advocates and, preferably, loyal, regular attendees.

Should we treat every guest the same? Yes and no. Some guests are much more valuable to you. Your VIPs desire and deserve special attention. However, all guests should be treated with respect. Developing guest loyalty pays off by making *all* guests feel special. They, in turn, will come more often, spend more and could become VIPs.

GUESTS FROM DIFFERENT GENERATIONS

There are a number of ways to look at classifying your guests, beginning with their generation. Most of us are aware of the different generations: Pre-war (born before 1945); Baby Boomers (born 1946–64); Gen X (born 1965–79); Gen Y/Millennials (born 1980–1995); Gen Z (born 1996–2009); and the new Gen Alpha (born after 2010). However, we must remember that all the individuals within these generations have their own distinct expectations, values and beliefs, based on their upbringing and experiences. So you cannot stereotype according to generation.

Baby Boomers are the largest segment of our guests today. Many have considerable disposable income, are retired or getting ready to retire and looking for new experiences. Many of these people in the past have avoided the gaming venue experience because it didn't speak to their needs or tastes at that time. The best food offering, for instance, was usually the bountiful bargain buffet, whereas Boomers generally have higher expectations and are looking for a more elegant experience. Today, some big venues are offering more than twenty different dining experiences, often including the traditional buffet, which is still a draw for some in this generation. This group have been our "meat and potatoes" for many years, but we have also got to be ready for the next wave, which will take our businesses forward.

GEN X, THE FORGOTTEN GENERATION (BORN 1965–79)

Don't forget about Gen X, the most forgotten and overlooked generation. This was the first generation to be hit by the tightening of employment in Western countries. These people have worked hard but will retire with less savings. It is also said that they are the first generation to earn less than their parents.

With high debt levels and low disposable income, this generation is typically looking for better deals and value for money.

GEN Y/MILLENIALS (BORN 1980-95)

Gen Y is the children of the Baby Boomers, many of whom are still living at home and have high disposable incomes. Gen Y will live longer and delay adulthood, marriage and having a family. For these people, "adolescence does not finish until the age of 30." Brought up in an age of computers and cell phones, they are more tech savvy and highly connected to their network of friends.

What they look for in a venue are areas where they can sit and meet their friends, a quality and convenient food offering and a wider variety of nontraditional beverages.

GEN Z (BORN 1996-2009)

Gen Z is known for being passionate, pragmatic and in control. These people have intensive, focused bursts of attention. They are driven by real and relevant interactions. For them, visuals are more important than words. Society has told them to be themselves, and that's exactly what they expect: a world that will adjust to their particular wants and needs. This is reiterated daily on social media where they share inspiring quotes urging them to be leaders—not followers—and to follow their passions and so on.

GEN ALPHA (BORN AFTER 2010)

Around 2030 a whole new generational group will arrive in our venues, Gen Alpha. It is worth considering, now, how we plan to engage this generation. With early access to amazing technology, it will be a waiting game to see what these people really need and expect from a venue.

A VENUE FOR ALL GENERATIONS

So how do you create a venue that appeals across all of these demographics? Younger generations need to start thinking of your venue as a place to go for a good time if you are going to make lifetime guests of them. Social games such as Candy Crush are very popular and could be seen as precursors to the gaming room. Social casino games make up most of the top twenty grossing apps on Facebook, with female players now representing 60% of the market. So how do you attract younger generations into your venue without alienating your regular Baby Boomer generation?

Designing a floor plan that will encourage a cross-section of generations is critical, and some of our highly successful venue managers have done this very well. They have basically segmented their large open floor space into multiple areas, defining them not with walls but as mini-environments to appeal to these varying demographics. For example, one section is a great-looking sports bar, with multiple big-screen TVs and high tables. Close by is a lounge area with comfortable club chairs and tables and featuring low-key live entertainment, typically a guitar duo and perhaps a DJ later in the evening. The open-plan dining area has three cuisine offerings and a mix of seating styles to suit and opens onto a wonderful outdoor area that has childrens play equipment under cover and a dining space and lounge chairs to relax in while listening to another group of musicians who are based outside. The gaming area with its spacious floor plan, both inside and out, provides the players a luxurious and exciting ambience. These different segments acknowledge generational differences and preferences without sacrificing the open feel. The food offerings are similarly differentiated, from a pizzeria to a noodle bar to an upmarket bistro with an awesome restaurant-quality menu. These venues have created welcoming areas that appeal to all generations and motivate guests to spend significant money and time there.

STATS

UN population studies have stated that in the year 2030 there will be more people in the world over 65 years of age than there will be under 5 years of age. Is your venue planning, now, how it is going to keep this group engaged or, more importantly, are you currently interacting with this group to create long-term relationships?

THE FEMALE FACTOR

According to world statistics there are more females in the world than males, so why is it that gaming venues have taken so long to take notice of these players in their venues? Some venue managers have learned more about their female guests through focus groups and surveys and have renovated and added new menu and entertainment choices in response to this analysis, including décor that is appealing to the eye with attractive colours, using a variety of textures and designs that are glamorous but also functional; lounges and low tables where groups can enjoy a selection of cocktails, boutique wines or even craft beers. Menu choices with smaller portions and healthy alternatives have encouraged men, as well, to start thinking about what they eat. Female players have a preference for gaming machines over the traditional casino card games. Gaming promotions and entertainment as well as gaming machines themed with well-liked television shows or movies should be aimed at the female market.

Females have driven the rise of the café culture, with their strong interest in quality coffee and teas, beautiful cake displays and comfortable café seating.

Female guests were overlooked for many years. However, the smart managers could see the rise in this group's attendance at their venues and improved all the facilities they used and not just the dining areas, as once thought. The growth in spending and loyalty from this group is certainly making an impact on their bottom line.

KNOWING WHO YOUR GUESTS ARE

In this era of Big Data, segmentation is increasingly used to classify guests. In the past, venues obtained basic information from guests, but now, it is far more comprehensive: how you prefer to be contacted, what language you speak at home, which foods you prefer and so on. All of this information is collected on the member database, including members' spending and visitation frequency.

Whilst gathering this data is important, using the data correctly is more important. The real trick is turning the collected data into action to match your guests' preferences with special offerings, events and tickets. One thing we have learned from gaming analysts is to not move machines around too often. People like to find "their" machine right where they left it. If you are introducing new machines, make sure you let people know about it. How your lines of machines are organised matters, too; people don't like feeling boxed in. Signage matters a lot; it is terribly frustrating for guests to have to look for fifteen minutes to find a restroom, for instance, or the way to the car park. Don't give them a reason to not come back.

THE BIG FOUR CATEGORIES OF GUESTS

Large or small, all venues serve four categories of guest: the Coveted High Roller; the Midlevel Regular; the Lower-Value Segment ("Churn and Burn") and the No-Value Guest. The number-one challenge is to attract and hang on to the Coveted High Rollers, because they are less likely to be as loyal as they used to be. The demographic of who they are has changed, but what they have in common is the strong desire to be recognised, rewarded and courted. Loyalty and membership programmes are one way to serve that set of needs but not the only way.

A. THE COVETED HIGH ROLLERS

Coveted High Rollers come in a variety of ages, genders, cultures and behavioural types. Venues often use card membership systems to recognise them. Sometimes it is the colour of the card that identifies the High Roller; sometimes the card has symbols, such as a jewel, key or flame, which indicate where you are on the tiered loyalty programme. However, listen and tailor the tier description to your guest. There are venues that no longer have the coloured card. Instead, they just use a symbol because some Coveted High Rollers felt their privacy was being compromised when other guests could easily see their tier classification from the card colour.

The top tier of Coveted High Rollers can be broken into three types in terms of their wants and behaviours. First, you have those who want to be seen and recognised by name by all the team members and expect to have their favourite gaming machine ready: the whole VIP treatment. Then there's the next group, still in that top tier, who still want to be acknowledged by team members and to enjoy all the fringe benefits of being High Rollers but don't necessarily need all the fuss and bother. Lastly, you have those who prefer to come in and be more or less anonymous. They are not interested in even a brief acknowledgement; they just want to go straight to their machines and play. It is critical to retain your highest-spending Coveted High Rollers. But how do you do it? Do you give them more shows, fancier rooms, more comps?

Here's another way of thinking about it: pay attention to the small things because, for these players, the small things may be a more impactful way to show that you care. One of our clients has an anonymous Coveted High Roller whom you would never recognise as a high-stakes player, given his rather shabby clothing and beat-up car. He was wooed to a competing casino but didn't care for the treatment he got there, which, presumably, reflected how the team members viewed him, and he quickly returned to his regular venue. Except for the most reclusive ones, Coveted High Rollers generally share a preference for being known and treated as special, and increasingly, we see VIP hosts at venues whose sole job is to spend quality time with High Rollers to get to know them better and pass on personal information to the gaming manager so these guests can be provided with suitable benefits.

A benefit kept as a secret or given begrudgingly by a team member is no benefit at all. You don't want your venue to be seen as stingy. Understand the link between honesty, generosity and your valued guests' loyalty so that your team can act upon information. For example, when one venue learned that a Coveted High Roller was going on a trip, their management team presented them with carry-on luggage as a gift, which was thoughtful and showed they were listening.

INSPIRING LOYALTY AND THE COVETED HIGH ROLLERS

Coveted High Rollers are courted with very special offers, including offers to their partners, keeping them occupied while the High Rollers are busy gambling. Partner privileges can include guided shopping tours or styling workshops. Many venues have day spas. Offering treatments to partners at your day spa is also a great way to get their loyalty as well as their partner's. You can often connect with a high-end retail store to bring a special fashion show to a small group of these high-value partners so that instead of taking them shopping, the shop comes to them. It is a great idea if your venue caters to these high-end guests and you are in an upscale urban area. You can also offer tickets to live sporting events or invitations to watch the "big screen" in a private room at your venue, with food and beverages to keep them entertained.

That strong rapport is critical, and the special treatment needs to begin as soon as the VIP guest arrives at your venue. The parking attendant who parks their car should be in contact with the gaming host, notifying them when the guest arrives. That the team makes sure that the guest's favourite machine is sparkling clean and that their beverage of choice is ready to be delivered as soon as they sit down. This makes them feel honoured without getting in the way of their play.

If you only ate sausages, potatoes and peas every night, you would eventually get bored, so don't worry too much if your Coveted High Roller should stray. If your product and service is consistently above their expectations, they will return.

A whole lot of interesting psychological research has been undertaken, especially on what we call the Flashy Factor. As we have noted, there are people who enjoy being seen, recognised and coddled. There are those who are more or less indifferent to that, and then there are others who don't feel comfortable with any level of recognition. Some people actually get extra enjoyment out of occasionally sneaking in, a sort of illicit buzz, if you like, from doing something that's a little bit naughty. A good concierge or VIP host can quickly classify the guests according to these preferences and build strong relationships with them.

THREE TYPES OF HIGH ROLLERS

LOVES TO BE SEEN

LIKES TO BE ACKNOWLEDGED

PREFERS PRIVACY

The staff should be aware of the guests' needs—for example, whether they like to chat or they just want to sit and play the gaming machine. Creating a welcome that is genuine, whether it is with a smile and a nod or verbally, is the key to making a connection with your guests. If you aren't attentive to these guests' needs, they will move on to a venue that is. Remember that they do talk to each other, no matter how much they like their privacy. Like a bad comment on Trip Advisor, a few words from a disgruntled Coveted High Roller could certainly have an impact on your bottom line.

B. MIDLEVEL REGULARS

In paying that special attention to the Coveted High Rollers, venues often make the mistake of ignoring that other vital segment, the midlevel player who's a regular guest and from among whose ranks will come tomorrow's Coveted High Roller. High Rollers are fickle, demanding and often spoiled, so there's a lot of value in looking after those in the next tier down, who may be more loyal. And given that they may be at your venue three or four times a week over the course of years, they deserve your attention.

What do they respond to? Just like most of your Coveted High Rollers, Midlevel Regulars enjoy being recognised for their loyalty and being accorded special treatment. Assigning them a VIP host and their new membership card reflecting their higher status creates in them a sense of being valued, which they hadn't had before as Midlevel Regulars. These new, "recognised" Midlevel Regulars will come more often. They will tell their friends, and they will bring more people with them. And it is far more likely that your gentle nudge will move them up in terms of what they spend with you, even into the top tier. They'll go from being "bridesmaids" to being "the bride".

In courting both these groups, the importance of an active and involved front-line VIP team can't be overstated. If you can't manage a full-time VIP host, you need to make sure that someone is tasked with that job each shift, because if you don't, your Coveted High Rollers and Midlevel Regulars are likely to be poached by your competitors.

TIP

Venues where these players are engaged individually by management seeking their response to suggested changes in facilities and offerings as well as décor and furnishings have been associated with increased loyalty, as these guests feel they play an important role at the venue and their comments and sug-gestions are noted and implemented wherever possible.

No matter which type of special guest they are, these players talk to each other and discuss the offerings and rewards of other venues.

C. LOWER-VALUE SEGMENT

The least loved segment of gaming is, of course, this tier, known by various nicknames including "Churn and Burn", "Coupon Clippers", and even "Spoon Stealers". But you do need these guests to make your venue feel alive, even if they are just there to play keno or bingo. How do you move them from the bingo room to the gaming room to perhaps the next tier level? During the break between games, try offering these guests a promotion or entertainment in the gaming room. This gives them a reason to stay and walk around when the bingo game's done.

Make sure you find a way to urge them to experience everything your venue has to offer, and you will move some of them up to that middle level. They will go home and tell friends and family how well they were treated, and you will find you get a whole new crop of guests who might otherwise never have come to your venue. Whether they are bingo players or whether they are mums out on a Tuesday at lunchtime because the venue has a face-painting artist and a clown for the kids, those people will come back on their own, start to become very loyal and begin to spend a lot more money in the venue.

Wouldn't you rather have fifty bingo bottoms on seats than fifty empty seats? Some venue managers complain that these guests fill up their car parks so the higher-value players can't find a place to park, but without them, you would often have a very dull venue, and nobody wants to come into an empty place.

Be aware, too, that by appealing to one group, you may inadvertently offend another. In one venue we know the management wanted to attract Gen Y males, so they put in a surfing game. It was very popular with the Gen Y guys, and they cheered each other on, quite noisily. The fallout, however, was that the Asian guests, whom the management wished to retain, were put off and, to some extent, intimidated by all the shouting, and they took their money elsewhere. Most venues work around this by having loud zones and quiet zones, areas where people play nosier games, and others where, mostly, the more solitary, quiet gamers just play their machines or play at tables, often for very high stakes. They don't want to be distracted.

D. NO-VALUE SEGMENT

There are some guests who add no value to your venue. In fact, their behavior actually drives guests away. They come to your venue to just sit at the bar; they have no interest in gaming at all. Their penchant is to sit there and give your guests the "Manhattan Once-Over". You know when you walk into the room, and you feel as if the air has been sucked out? With not a sound to be heard, all eyes are upon you, monitoring your every move. It is like walking into a redneck bar. Some venues throw up a wall of plants or a half wall so these guests can't glare at the incoming guests or find another way to marginalise them. Unfortunately, some venues have long-term team members who have struck up relationships with these guests and have become toxic. Sometimes, relocating these team members will do the trick.

You are likely to have to deal in the same way with what we call Change Haters and Complainers. These guests believe it is their right to quiz every decision made on the premises. From "their" table, which they have chosen for its direct view of the entrance, they scrutinise each guest entering the venue. We call tables where these guests sit "tables of knowledge". These Change Haters and Complainers are always loud, stare rudely at non-regulars and complain loudly to the staff when the television channel is changed from their favourite sporting programme. Again, these guests can make your venue seem unwelcoming and even hostile to new guests. They need to be moved or discouraged, as must any team members who accommodate their behaviour.

THE RISE OF THE DRAGON MARKET GUESTS

There are many ways to let your Asian guests know they are welcome. You can start by having staff who speak their language wear special badges that identify them. It can mean decorating with red and gold, which are seen as lucky colours. Using the number eight as much as possible is attractive, too. Like most of us, Asian guests are attracted to the luxury experience. And you can't think only in terms of the Chinese guest; we see more and more Korean, Vietnamese and other Asian ethnicities now entering our venues. That said, the Chinese remain the dominant culture in so far as gambling is concerned.

Guests from Asia may enjoy drinking games at the bar in which the host throws the dice. (This may not be allowed by law in some venue locations.) They are fond of karaoke and like to have gaming machines in the karaoke room, rather than off in another area. We have talked earlier about Feng Shui. Just to restate: if you don't pay attention to the rules that govern this in your layout, rest assured that your error will be noticed and your Asian guests will go elsewhere to play.

DRAGON TIP

One thing we have noticed over the years: if you provide your guests with an upscale experience, they will rise to that level. If you roll out the red carpet and wow them even before they enter the venue, they will be far more likely to dress, act and spend accordingly. This is particularly true of the guests from Asia, who will feel honoured by your provision of a first-class experience especially for them.

CHAPTER 3

VIP Leadership

The Tale Of The Tortoise And Rabbit—Being A Superior Leader To Grow Your Team Talent

Mantra: The team is the reflection of
the mindset of the leader.

ARE YOU A RABBIT OR A TORTOISE?

There are a lot of leadership styles out there. Two we are very familiar with are what we call the Rabbit and the Tortoise. The Rabbit is typically chaotic, overwhelmed and running around. They are trying to do too many things at once, because, on some level, they think they have to have a hand in every piece of the business. They neglect to delegate, which means they don't really know who's in charge of the "troops," and when asked, they are always busy.

The opposite is the Tortoise, who has a methodical approach, considers the team and understands their strengths. They are more  inclusive and all about cheering and bringing the team on the journey. The Tortoise has discovered that including others makes them stronger, not weaker, and they build and grow strong executive teams, seeing the potential each individual brings to the table.

Successful Tortoises are always happy to share their ideas on how they run their business, because their mantra is, "If I show you what we have done, and you can do it, too, then that benefits everyone."

Today's CEOs are a group of very smart businessmen and women who have MBAs. Many worked in the industry whilst studying and, on completion, stayed in the industry. They are true professionals, run their venue as a business and are less likely to run one-man shows. They understand the importance of team building and sharing their vision with the executive team in order to maximise buy-in.

STEP-BY-STEP WINS

So how do you develop leaders? It is about promoting ability, not tenure. It is looking for that person in your organisation who has that glint in their eye, who's fully engaged and soaking up learning like a sponge. It is about developing these potential leaders by giving them a spot on your team and the opportunity to grow into bigger and better roles. The young leaders of today want to be challenged with opportunities for growth within the venue and industry.

The smart leaders tell their managers, "I will give you as much opportunity to learn as you want. You just soak it up, but I also realise that you are not going to be here for the rest of your career, because staying in one place isn't going to make you a great leader. Even though I have put the time and effort into developing you, you now need to go from my venue to another venue to gain further experience. Hopefully, you will eventually come back more seasoned and knowledgeable." It is that sense of sharing across the industry that differentiates a visionary leader from a small-minded one. The attitude used to be, "I'm not going to put my time and effort into developing you, because you are going to leave in two or three years' time." That sort of mentality is not there with these successful leaders. They want to build their managers up and help them get a job somewhere else to improve their journey.

A smart leader encourages employees to better themselves, perhaps to continue their education or complete advanced degrees. Some venues subsidise the cost with the understanding that the employees will stay with the venue for a set period of time afterward. Some smart leaders are using the Lombardo and Eichinger 70/20/10 blended learning model to maximise their training. This means that employees are spending 70% of their time in on-the-job learning outside their comfort zone, 20% of their time in mentoring and coaching with their leader, and 10% of their time in taking formal education courses and reading.

A great way to develop your leadership team is through the allocation of Manager Portfolios, which pertain to strategic roles with additional responsibilities covering different aspects of the venue. They help new leaders better understand the systems, procedures and regulatory compliance affecting the whole business. Having these portfolios really gets them seeing the business from a different viewpoint. Not every venue offers portfolios, but the ones that do very often have the best multi-skilled managers.

Some managers lock themselves in an ivory tower, not sharing their vision and preferring to manage from their office. Contrast that with smart leaders at successful venues: each day when the doors open, the CEO and the executive team stand at the entry points and are scattered inside the venue at key locations to welcome the guests. We know not everyone has a gregarious personality, but welcoming efforts like this have made a difference in the way that guests view management teams. Instead of conveying the idea that they are focused solely on revenue, managers come across as caring individuals who are making that guest connection face to face. This is a great example of "leading from the front", and sets the tone for the whole team. There are many managers and leaders who ignore team members as they walk past them, and they are the ones with workplace culture problems. VIP leaders know nearly all of their team by name and walk around greeting and checking in regularly. By varying their routines every day, they can see different teams in action and come up with new and innovative ideas.

PLAYING ABOVE THE LINE: THE BEHAVIOURS OF VIP LEADERS

The behaviour of every leader is always a choice. Those who take responsibility and are accountable for their own decisions, right or wrong, and who are willing to make the choices are at the top, acting as leaders. On the other hand, those who are into denial, blaming or justification tend to struggle with the leadership role, procrastinate and remain unfulfilled. Being decisive is also important. As Yoda (from *Star Wars*) said, "There is no try; there is do or do not." Stop trying and start doing. Leaders make mistakes, admit them and recover quickly.

In many organisations these behaviours are referred to as being "above the line" or "below the line". An easy acronym for remembering and teaching the key leadership behaviours is ROAD, which stands for Responsibility, Ownership, Accountability, and Decisiveness. Below the line are the behaviours not becoming of a leader: BED, which stands for Blame, Excuses and Denial. Imagine a diagram with a line across the middle, "ROAD" at the top and "BED" underneath. Those who fall below the line deny there are any problems; they make excuses, and they blame others while avoiding making decisions themselves. Getting people to take accountability, ownership and responsibility is playing above the line.

In stressful situations and when a leader's energy level is low, some leaders tend to fall back to "below-the-line" behaviours. That's weak leadership, so the plan is to stay in a high-energy state that keeps you above the line. You can lead by example and also remind other team members to choose "above-the-line" behaviours in those stressful times.

CHOOSE YOUR BEHAVIOR
STAY ABOVE THE LINE

UNDERSTANDING EACH MANAGER'S VALUES TO BUILD A VIP TEAM

We have found, when working with management teams, that it is all about understanding their value system, because if you're not working to your true self and being true to the values that you hold, then you're always searching for something else and trying to be someone you're not. There are five personal values that are key for VIP leaders:

1. Teamwork

2. Honesty

3. Accountability

4. Trustworthiness

5. Ambition

One value that doesn't get talked about openly is ambition. Without ambition as a driver, managers might be tempted to remain where they are comfortable.

In our Leadership Team Development programme, we work closely with attendees to identify and understand their own values and the values of others. Occasionally we see teams that don't have a single value in common, which produces nothing but anarchy. No team members work together; they all undermine each other. The staff members pick sides, and eventually, the CEO has to make the decision about who needs to go, because it is very hard to change the personal value systems of these team members. You might bring them around for a while, but ultimately, they will revert to their own core values. It is not a question of their being right or wrong. Rather, it is a question of them being congruent with their workplace, and some people are just never going to be the "right fit".

BEHAVIOURAL VALUES

We all have a set of core values, things that are fundamentally important to us. These values, which are sometimes called interests, are the underlying beliefs and principles that we carry around with us every single day.

Being aware of the fact that values are common behavioural motivators gives you greater insight into why certain conflicts happen.

People don't just have one core value; they have a set of values with varying degrees of importance. Take a moment to select your top eight core values from the following list.

Acceptance	Equality	Order
Accomplishment	Family	Peace
Accountability	Freedom	Pride
Ambition	Friendship	Privacy
Autonomy	Harmony	Recognition
Comfort	Honesty	Reputation
Competence	Honour	Respect
Control	Inclusion	Responsibility
Cooperation	Independence	Safety
Courage	Innovation	Security
Creativity	Integrity	Stability
Dignity	Leadership	Teamwork
Efficiency	Loyalty	Trust

After working with many VIP team members over the decades, these are the top five values that are common to many of them:

1. Friendship

2. Respect

3. Responsibility

4. Teamwork

5. Honesty

VIP teams that have similar values strive together toward common goals.

VIP LEADERS DEVELOP OTHERS

VIP leaders understand the value of developing others and building leadership talent in their venue and the industry. We recommend undertaking a Values and Behavioural Analysis with your whole team in order to improve understanding and engagement. Are leaders born, or are they made? Some of these leaders are "accidental" leaders who grow into their roles very well if they are willing to seek advice from more experienced mentors and to learn as they step into the limelight. Most mentors are happy to talk to you if they truly know that you are there because you want to develop yourself. The best leaders are those who are willing to help the next group up after them.

What works? Being a beacon, being positive, looking for the good in people and letting them know you see it. That's how you ignite the potential in others. You have got to be willing and able to ask for help. And you have to be ready to check and lose your prejudices.

The Hard Rock Café has an interesting motto: "Love All, Serve All". It is a good way for leaders to think. It is important to check and lose your preferences/prejudices and not be racist, sexist, age-ist or tech-ist. Not everyone understands the power and strength you get with diversity, with listening to opposing or different points of view and giving them your consideration. If everyone were the same, we would never move forward, though, admittedly, we are wired to like those who are like us.

While we need to share common values, how we come at them is going to be different for each of us, and that's a great thing when you are building a team. There's a place for everyone to bring his or her strengths, and they are all to be valued.

When all venues offer similar entertainment, beverages and dining options, the only difference is service. As a leader, you need to know your values and build relationships with your team, understanding their values so that they will build relationships with your guests. Understanding workplace behaviour through staff values achieves a higher connection with guests.

HOW TO SHIFT POOR ATTITUDES

There are many things that can cause a team member to have a poor attitude or *disengagement,* including personal issues, health issues, family troubles and workplace disputes. Avoid jumping to premature conclusions; always first make a gentler enquiry about any problems or concerns that you have noticed. Start with phrases like "We seem to be having an issue with …" and "Tell me more about what happened …"

Smart leaders always lead by example and start by improving their own attitude. Be a shining beacon of positivity, optimism and tough love. "Mood contagion" starts with the leader and spreads amongst the team quickly. Avoid any "below-the-line" behaviours like blame, excuse or denial (BED). Do the most you can to find out what you really like about team members. Find and focus on what they do well. A team member's poor attitude can actually be shifted when you focus on that person's strengths and develop them with positive feedback. Everyone has a flame of potential inside. What gets rewarded gets repeated. This re-engagement strategy is called, "fanning the flame".

Another great way to shift a poor attitude is by refocussing your conversations on what the team member thinks about. Anything you can do to boost the personal energy level of these team members will help them view things in a more positive way. Start an attitude shift by talking about positive things, possibilities, the future, flexibility, things we can do and so on.

CONVERSATIONS THAT SHIFT ATTITUDES
Move your focus from
- Negative to positive: help people to start seeing their positive side.
- Past to future: help people who are stuck in the past to look to the future.
- Fixed to flexible: help people to move beyond their comfort zones.
- Impossible to possible: help people who are pessimistic to see other possibilities.
- Can't to can: help people to accept what can't be done and find what can be done.
- Me/you to we: help people to be inclusive of others and part of the team.

SHIFTING YOUR OWN ATTITUDE: PERSONAL RE-ENGAGEMENT TECHNIQUES

It is important to stay positive, honest and open, even in stressful times. Keep your focus on finding and focussing on the good: personal bests, small wins and any positive achievements. Learn about developing your own optimism (see Martin Seligman's book *Learned Optimism*) and consider taking or offering happiness/positivity training.

You can become a more effective leader by choosing to ask better questions to focus on the positive to engage and re-engage your team members.

QUESTIONS THAT FOCUS ON THE POSITIVE TO ENGAGE OTHERS

INSTEAD OF SAYING	SAY THIS TO FOCUS ON THE POSITIVE AND OPTIMISTIC
How are things?	What's working for you?
How's it going?	What's gone well today?
How are you?	What's the best thing?
What's happening?	
What are you up to?	What are you happy about?
Where are we?	What can we celebrate?
What are you unhappy about?	What are you grateful for?
Why are you so upset?	
What's happened?	What are you looking forward to?
	What's next?
	What's the next step?

Instead of discussing things that can't be done, ask—	What can we do?
	What is possible?
	What could you do?
Instead of asking, "What's going on? What's the problem?", ask—	What solutions and ideas do we have?
	Let's see. What can we do?
Don't use the words *I/me* & *you*.	Use more of the words *we/us* and less of the word *I*.
Don't label team members with bad names.	

THE LOVE BUCKET MODEL FOR ENGAGING AND ENERGISING

Engaged team members are far more productive than those who are under-engaged or disengaged. They work harder, have less sick days and less injury claims and are far more likely to be retained long term and develop into leaders. One of the most powerful tools for leaders is the use of genuine praise and appreciation. Surveys have found that most team members feel under-appreciated in the workplace, and as yet, no one has ever died of over-appreciation!

The Love Bucket is a simple technique to improve engagement and energise your team. Every person has a love bucket inside. Happy and engaged team members have a love bucket that is nearly full. Unhappy or disengaged team members have a bucket that is nearly empty.

In addition to praise and appreciation, team members like rewards and recognition. Some just like special individual attention and time with *you*, a leader they trust and respect. You can make use of these love languages to fill up their love bucket and boost their energy and engagement levels for the highest team performance.

FILL 'ER UP! FILL UP THEIR LOVE BUCKET USING THESE LOVE LANGUAGES

- Praise for effort: use more positive affirmations like "You did ..."
- Appreciation: appreciate team members (e.g., "Thanks for ...!"
- Rewards: provide recognition and other rewards.
- Touch: give high fives and pats on the back.
- You: devote quality time and your attention to team members.

GIVING GREAT FEEDBACK: AVOID SARCASM!

Another great tip when giving any positive feedback to team members is to be specific (not general), truthful (avoid puffery), original (avoid repetition), timely (avoid delaying positive feedback) and energetic (avoid giving begrudging feedback). An easy way to remember this is through the acronym *STORE,* for storing more energy in their love bucket. If you want your praise and appreciation to be well received by team members, the best thing you can do is to eradicate any sarcasm in your workplace. Sarcasm is a passive-aggressive behaviour and not beneficial to harmonious working relations. In some teams, sarcasm is rife and what is worse is that it may start with the leadership team. Make a sustained effort to put an end to sarcasm in your workplace and avoid making sarcastic comments yourself. Use genuine praise and appreciation instead and see your teamwork and productivity improve.

PLUG ANY LEAKS IN TEAM MEMBERS' LOVE BUCKETS: EASE MY PAIN!

For some team members, praise and appreciation doesn't work well. If their love bucket is leaky, it needs to be fixed. We need to reduce their pain. Find out what is causing the leak. Ask some enquiring questions like, "If there were one thing we could do to help you do a better job or make your job easier, what would it be?" or "What really cheeses you off, and how can we prevent it from happening?" Sometimes you will discover the real reason for their disengagement, and it may be outside the workplace. Ignoring the problem usually causes it to get worse. Remember that counselling poor performance in the workplace can help a team member succeed.

THE "TOUGH LOVE" STRATEGY: BECOMING A DISCIPLINED LEADER

Team members like a workplace that is fair. They do not like other team members doing the wrong thing and not being held to account. You need to be a strong yet compassionate leader to maintain workplace discipline, like being a "steel fist in a velvet glove".

You can be a strong leader by setting the standard and being accountable and holding others to account. Clearly spell out to the team the house rules for induction and counselling, especially prior to recruitment. Learn how to give effective negative feedback, too. Study tough conversations (calling poor behaviours). Disciplinary action (loss of bonus, etc.), warnings and, finally, terminations have to be an option.

VIP leaders create a disciplined culture by outlining a code of conduct and setting high expectations; goals and targets are set, both agreed targets and stretch targets. There are also clear consequences. This promotes responsibility and accountability. Push beyond your comfort zone; you learn best in the "learning zone", just outside your comfort level. Work on changing habits with practice. "Drills make skills."

STEPPING UP FROM BUDDY TO BOSS

Often a less-than-optimal management style can be turned around with tailored coaching. Too often, a staff member is given the "tap on the shoulder", so to speak, and is moved up the ladder with little or no support in acquiring management or leadership techniques. These new managers are thrown into a situation in which they want to prove the Executive Managers made the right choice in promoting them while watching their back as shunned team members wait for them to make a wrong move so they can gloat that the Executive Managers made the wrong choice. We all know team members like to divide and conquer managers.

A venue has to have a unified management team, transcending all areas, including the Executive Chef. All managers need to know they have the support of their peers. Smart managers arrange times to meet and perhaps even call upon a facilitator to mediate a discussion of current happenings and work toward the Action Plan.

We have witnessed team unity when this has been done, particularly with Front Line and Back of House Managers and Executive Chefs. Their purpose is strengthened and results are achieved more quickly when they know they can depend on each other and the flow of communication is open.

Some people really aren't comfortable with the shift from working *in* the business instead of *on* the business, with being a supervisor or leader as opposed to being a front-line team member. Another problem you see is people struggling with what are called espoused values versus lived values. In other words, they say one thing but do another. There are also going to be differences depending on where staff are in the chain of command, whether they are the CEO, COO, CFO, or Department Head. Human Resources, Marketing and Finance personnel, Duty Managers and even Team Leaders/Supervisors who have just begun their management journey all see things slightly differently. In order to align their viewpoints, you must have some aligned values.

Usually, staff in all those different roles value slightly different things: The HR Department usually values people and performance. The Sales and Marketing Department values styles and competition. The Finance Department values accuracy, precision and compliance. The Technology Department values technology, sometimes rather more than people. The Operations Manager and the CEO are the ones who are trying to pull it all together and steer the team in the right direction. Common core values can keep everyone moving in the same direction and build trust and cooperation between these management silos.

Team building activities outside the workplace can be a great tool to pull these diverse personalities together, but the activities need to be carefully chosen, because, sometimes, they can devolve into competitions rather than cooperative exercises.

LEADING A CULTURALLY DIVERSE TEAM

Teams today are increasingly diverse, hailing from many different countries, ethnic groups and cultures. Each has its own set of values, and as long as they are all aligned, that works out fine. But sometimes you will have conflicts in the workplace because of cultural values that may not be aligned.

Being sensitive to these differences and helping people from diverse backgrounds work well together is key to good VIP leadership. Opportunities to optimise teamwork and working toward the same goals meet with great success. It is important for all those involved in the team to feel that they are safe and that each one is heard. It is when ethnic cultural values differ that problems may arise, undermining the workplace culture, goals and objectives. Differences may not always be "personal" but stem, rather, from how we each approach life, given our different values. As a leader, begin with the requirement of mutual respect and make sure you model that respect for your entire team.

Effective, intelligent leadership is key to good management both at the top—the CEO—and at the level of the middle management team tasked with leading the troops.

CEOs should be aware and on top of the cultural shifts affecting their business, because leading the culture change starts with the CEO. Real leaders are at their best when things are at their worst. We have seen some magnificent leaders who particularly stand out when the pressure is on. Anybody can be a great leader and inspiring when everything's going well, when the bonus checks are coming through and when the money is flowing through the doors. We know clients who have only had to unlock their doors and the crowds arrived, the money came in, and it was as simple as that. They didn't have to do much as their competition was below par, so they were the standouts. It's easy to lead in good times; it's the turbulent times that test good leaders.

CHAPTER 4

VIP Team Members

Skunks Or Puppy Dogs?
Overcoming The Many Challenges
Of Building A VIP Team

Mantra: If you want to go fast, go alone. If
you want to go far, go as a VIP team.

WHAT MAKES A VENUE SUCCESSFUL?

There are a number of factors that have an impact on your guests'
satisfaction and experience, but none are more critical than your
team. The attitudes, appearance and service ethic of those who
interact daily and directly with guests are the human "face" in
your venue. Over the years in the business, we have seen a real
change in the attitudes of team members, from the old-style
attitude of "You are just lucky I'm even standing here at the cash
register" to the new and improved, more guest-oriented culture
that today's guests demand. Guests want information; they want
a warm welcome, staff who are ready and eager to answer their
questions, point them in the right direction and make them feel
valued. If they don't receive that VIP treatment, chances are they
will go elsewhere.

So how do you raise the level of service at your venue and engage your employees as stakeholders in change? The first step of smart leaders is to interact with and communicate regularly with management and team members. If you are not living the values and setting the standard of service by engaging your team, they can't follow, and your culture won't improve.

The next step is establishing what your corporate values are. Creating a benchmark for how team members are expected to behave makes it clear who is a good cultural fit for your organisation, and who will be trained up to meet the standards you are setting or leave if they can't or won't be congruent with those values. Building a team with aligned values is not a quick fix; perseverance and persistence is required to get the best from your team.

To make workplace cultural change last, it is vitally important to get all the team members engaged so that nobody feels left out. You can't afford to have clashing sets of values and expectations, because if you cannot agree on what is important, then change and progress will be limited. You need to have champions in your team who have bought into the change, as ultimately, they will be the drivers of that change. There has to be a respectful, supportive attitude rather than a punitive attitude toward those who find change challenging. When staff members don't pull their weight, your Change Champion has to feel confident enough to not confront that individual but rather to say, "Come on. I can help you make this job go a lot quicker", if, say, the job is collecting glasses or cleaning ashtrays at the end of the night. That Change Champion also has to be willing to go to the supervisor or manager when necessary and say, "Look, we have had a really good shift, but this person's just not working and it's not fair, so they need to be brought in for a discussion about their work." This Change Champion is not a whistle blower but rather a team player who thinks of the collective group and the guests who may be affected. Be proactive about identifying the team member— the Skunk—no one wants to work with.

THE SKUNK AND THE PUPPY DOG: ALL ABOUT ATTITUDE

Team members fall into one of two categories when it comes to attitudes, personality and work ethic: Skunks or Puppy Dogs.

THE SKUNK: THE ODOUR OF POOR ATTITUDE

In nature, the skunk is known to spray its offensive odour over a wide area when feeling threatened, affecting all that are nearby, not just the target. In the workplace, the Skunks' poor attitude is reflected in their behaviour, which has an impact on team morale and guest experience. You can spot the Skunks when they come to work. They shuffle their feet with their heads down, and when other staff members call out, "Good morning!", they either grunt in reply or ignore them completely. Usually, Skunks are late, never on time to relieve a coworker. Skunks take their sweet time signing in and don't care about coworkers who are waiting for them and who may have to pick the kids up from school or have another commitment to attend to and are now cranky because the Skunks are late. The whole team's mood and attitude take a hit when the Skunks come in. Just the prospect of working with a Skunk is a downer, because the Skunk's attitude is "It is all about *me*."

As a team member, when you walk in the door of your venue, you are onstage. The lights come on and your smile has to be there, regardless of what happened to you that morning, because hospitality is not just an industry; it's an attitude! Skunks don't see it that way, and their mood pulls everyone down around them. What is more disappointing is Skunks don't recognise or take responsibility for their mood.

Skunks are the ones who do not work as fast as they could. They are careless about safety and leave objects around that might cause another team member to be injured. You have undoubtedly been served by a Skunk at some point and wondered how that person got a job on the front line. When Skunks take your money, they may not even bother to make eye contact with you. For them, it's strictly a transaction. A Skunks' poor attitude affects not only their coworkers but ultimately, your guests, too. That "stink" spreads, and now all the guests who encounter the Skunk at your venue are wishing they had stayed at home.

Nobody wants to be a Skunk. And it's almost impossible to turn Skunks into good coworkers and team members, because they are simply not built that way. Skunks are comfortable with their consistent unhappiness.

THE PUPPY DOG

Puppy Dogs are the opposite of Skunks. They are keen, enthusiastic and energetic. They are eager, wanting to improve and are there to support you. They may make mistakes as everyone does but are grateful to learn and happy to review procedures until they get them right. Guests love them because they are eager to engage with them, thanks to their friendly, outgoing nature. Predictably, Puppy Dogs annoy Skunks. When Puppy Dogs come bouncing in, Skunks say things such as, "What are you on, happy pills?" or "What's your problem?" When Skunks work with Puppy Dogs, they try and pull them down to their level, and sometimes, they succeed. Very often, Puppy Dogs resign, because they just don't like the workplace culture and choose not to be a Skunk. Don't let this happen!

You know the best team members communicate the benefits of the venue. They take the time to know a little more about their regular guests and ask how they are feeling if they have been ill, or they ask how their grandkids are. According to our industry surveys, the relationships that great team members have with their guests makes all the difference in how your venue stacks up against your competition. Their smiles and welcoming attitude are what keeps guests coming back.

THE MOST MEMORABLE CONCIERGES AND WHAT MAKES THEM GREAT

Over the years, we have met and worked with some amazing front door/foyer team members. No matter what time of day or night it is, these shining stars are always smiling and welcoming. Even if the guest before you was aggressive or abusive, you will never see the signs of this because these staff members never share that mood with the next guest.

Their grooming is impeccable, and they wear an invisible badge of workplace pride.

They recognise each and every team member and guest. When they encounter guests they don't know, they take the time to welcome them personally and find out more about them. If they make a personal recommendation to guests entering the venue, they remember to ask about it when the same guests leave. They are proactive and don't wait for guests to ask; they anticipate questions.

It is this type of team member who makes the all-important first impression on your guests and will have them returning and referring others to your venue.

BUILDING A TEAM, NOT A GROUP OF INDIVIDUALS

What counts when it comes to team building? The teams we see working well on the floor are those in which every member understands the roles of each other. If one team member doesn't perform their role correctly, it creates a domino effect.

For example, a cashier at a register has given the wrong change repeatedly throughout their shift and is over or under at the end of the night, so how do team members handle this situation? Some team members don't care because they just want to go home, and they walk off leaving the problem for someone else to find. What they don't realise or care about is that the shift manager has to find the money and solve the problem, which may take hours. In the past, there wasn't much accountability for discrepancies, but now a note will be filed about that discrepancy on the team member's record. If it happens more than a set number of times, the team member receives a written warning, which can ultimately lead to termination. Sometimes the hospitality and gaming industry attracts dishonest people, especially when large amounts of money are involved; this is why accountability and precautionary steps need to be enforced.

THE TWELVE CHALLENGES OF BUILDING A VIP TEAM

In order to build an outstanding VIP Team, you need to solve twelve key challenges:

1. THE CHALLENGE OF RECRUITING A VIP TEAM

Many team-building challenges can be solved before they happen with quality recruiting. Too often, what you see is "warm body recruitment": if you turn up at the front door, you are hired. Recruit with the end result in mind and never in desperation. Your focus should be on hiring people and retaining them for at least two years, because the expenses associated with replacing unsatisfactory team members can really add up when you factor in the costs of training a replacement. The bottom line is if in doubt, throw them out; if they are not up to speed in terms of work and attitude during the probationary period, they are probably about as good as they are ever going to get.

While most savvy venues now understand the value of having applicants undergo a professional personality assessment or behavioural profile when they hire management team members, assessing the personalities of prospective front-line team members doesn't usually include that kind of assessing and profiling. There are ways within the perimeters of practicality to get a better idea of a candidate's people skills through the interview process. Many venues will begin with a group interview with as many as ten or fifteen in the room. They have the candidates play various kinds of cooperative games, while the managers look on from the sidelines and see how they interact with each other. Are they quiet or gregarious, cooperative or withdrawn? Usually there's a secondary process that allows you to see how the shyer, quieter candidates deal with other kinds of challenges. Those who make the cut are asked back for an individual interview.

The location of your venue can also make hiring a challenge if your staff members are not able to get there via public transport or the roadways are congested.

TIP
1. Use personality/behavioural profiling.
2. Find a local community of workers.
3. Build a team car park based away from the venue with private bus transportation or encourage the practice of car-pooling.

2. THE CHALLENGE OF ASSESSING CANDIDATES

The first thing to look at in candidates is how they present themselves in terms of appearance. Are they clean, appropriately dressed, nails in good order? Once, years ago, we interviewed a young woman who'd come to apply for a position as an apprentice chef. She was wearing a wet bikini and sandals. She'd thrown a skirt on, but her hair was wet and just tied loosely back. What was she thinking?

If job candidates don't learn the simple rules of your grooming policy, and they wear something out of line with that policy, that's clearly a stop sign. If they show up chugging a soda or don't bother to turn off their cell phone, it's clear they are not really focused on being there.

In the hospitality industry, long hair should always be worn pulled neatly back. So many people today have tattoos, and each venue has it's own grooming policy depending on their guests and management, allowing them either to show them or have them covered.

When you fail to correctly assess new hires, it shows up in your statistics in three months; that's all the time it takes for your carefully built operation to go off the rails. When your culture takes a hit, your service takes one, too. The questions asked of candidates at job interviews, and the person who is doing the asking are clearly key. And don't forget that bad hires will often drive off good team members, because who wants to work with a Skunk with a poor work ethic? They may not tell you the reason they are leaving, but they will leave. We saw it happen at one venue where the management changed the interviewing process without thinking it through, and by the time we had identified the problem through our reports, three months had passed, costing the venue a great deal of money and time in training new recruits whose values were not congruent with other team members or the venue's workplace culture.

TIP

1. Carry out reference checks. Contact past employers, not necessarily candidates' referees.

2. Involve candidates' prospective managers or supervisors in the hiring process.

3. Actively manage and assess during the probation period

3. THE CHALLENGE OF SELECTING AND INDUCTING YOUR VIP TEAM

Australia has fairly rigid workplace rules that include workplace assessments over a probationary period of six months. In a large venue with perhaps hundreds of team members, the middle management and team leaders have to be very mindful of assessing new front-line team members. Assessments of new recruits should also involve experienced team members providing feedback to managers. If the new hires don't work out, either dismissal or retraining needs to happen very quickly. Otherwise, you will find yourself saddled with recalcitrant or unreliable team members who, after that six-month period, may simply decide to turn up for work when it suits them. At that point, trying to figure out who ought to have been responsible for spotting the problem earlier is a waste of time. Much better to begin with the correct induction, the correct training and thorough, regular and timely follow-up assessments that include clear feedback to that probationary team member. Venues lose a lot of good team members when those employees feel they have just been thrown into the deep end and nobody's helped them. They will move to a venue where they do feel respected and valued and where their fellow team members not only share their values but also support them in the practical demands of the job.

Smart management provide great training and support to all team members, commencing with a full introduction to the venue and the workplace culture. Introducing new hires to the team, and seeing that they learn the specific ways in which management expect them to fulfil their role. Encourage questions and be sure to provide ongoing support through the training period, not showing them once and abandoning them.

TIP

1. Training and assessing on a continual basis
2. Full introduction of venue facilities on the first day
3. Buddy system with another staff member

4. THE CHALLENGE OF DEALING WITH YOUNGER TEAM MEMBERS

There are also some challenges in turning the new generation of workers into happy team players. Some university/college students have their parents' support and don't need to work, however, they choose to. Even those who have to work want to feel they have made a meaningful, personal workplace choice and have chosen your venue because they have heard what a great place it is to work in. When we talk to younger team members about why they chose a particular venue, we commonly hear, "I've got a friend who works here" or "We have been coming here for a few years and the staff always look really happy." These younger team members don't bond to a workplace in the way that their parents did. It used to be that you could expect someone who was comfortable with the job to spend years working for you, perhaps even through their whole career. The younger generation of team members may only stay put for a couple of years before moving on to the next job. They expect quicker promotions, without working their way through the ranks, but they often bring great, fresh ideas with them, and in common with older colleagues who are re-entering the workforce, can be great promoters for the new workplace culture you are creating.

TIP

1. Give them the opportunity to lead, and bring that positive attitude to their roles rather than simply promoting team members to the position of team leader on tenure.

2. Allow them to question the sacred cows in the business. You may be surprised by their answers.

3. Give them recognition and job titles.

5. THE CHALLENGE OF BUILDING A MULTICULTURAL TEAM

Another challenge to your corporate value system can crop up when you are merging two venues. How do the team members accept the amalgamation? How do they adjust to working together? We often find that companies with two venues, even if they are on opposite sides of the same town, can have two totally different sets of expectations for their guests and their team. It is imperative that the workplace culture, as well as your systems and processes, are the same across your brand, no matter how different your locations are. We have certainly seen brands struggle. In one case, the culture changed from a sporting venue that was very Anglo-Saxon to a venue that had a predominance of Asian guests. In that case, there were practical challenges to be addressed. Management had to look at recruiting bar and gaming team members who spoke a variety of languages and who also had the skill set for working in a hospitality venue. Those qualities don't always come in one package. An understanding of the various cultures within your team is critical for team harmony. An issue that we have come across arises when team members speak to each other in a language that is common to them but not to the other team members, making others feel alienated and anxious, as they feel they are being talked about. Management has to agree on a policy that is acceptable to all team members.

TIP
1. Be culturally sensitive and aware.
2. Be respectful and lead by example.
3. Avoid labelling people and stereotyping diverse groups.

6. THE CHALLENGE OF CREATING A WORKPLACE OF CHOICE

You are probably a lot more conscious now than in the past about how you look after your team, not only in terms of security but also in terms of how your venue shows respect for all staff. Have you had a look at your staff room lately? You provide your guests with beautiful décor and food and all these fantastic offerings, but when you look at staff rooms, they are often abominable, tiny rooms with broken furniture, sometimes used as dumping places for Christmas decorations and other seasonal decorations. It is a space that very few team members would go to relax between shifts or during breaks, and there's no excuse for that.

Smart venues provide comfortable, beautiful staff rooms, with free or subsidised meals for team members on shift. There are secure places for team members to store their belongings, free soft drinks, television and maybe even a pool table. We have heard some venue leaders say, "Why would you provide them with all of that? They will just turn it into a pigsty!" But what we have seen is that if you give your team an area that is clean with pleasant surroundings, they will respect it.

You can also use the staff room to help build company unity. We have seen photo walls where new team members have their photos posted with a short personal introduction like, "Hi, I'm Shelly. I'm studying law at Sydney Uni, and I have a Labrador puppy." It helps create relationships and a sense of teambuilding. We have brought that idea to several venues, and it's made a difference in morale, creating a positive upbeat feeling.

That's the essence of how to make your venue that workplace of choice, one at which people choose to work because they love what they do, and they really enjoy both the people they work with and the people they are there to serve. Public recognition of a good deed gets everyone feeling good and motivated. This is what is truly behind really good team members; they feel good when they do something good. They don't do something good to get a pat on the back; they do it for that internal reward, and they transfer their positive feelings to the guests.

TIP

1. Encourage team member relationships and community, which improves team morale and unity.

2. Work on the improvement of team member facilities and amenities.

3. Celebrate team member news and milestones in a team member newsletter.

7. THE CHALLENGE OF CONTINUOUS IMPROVEMENT

Getting team members who are comfortable in their fixed routines to change can be a challenge. Consider creating a competition for your team members to encourage buy-in and engagement. Seek their ideas, create change champions and praise any improvement.

As you are aware, membership renewal season can be overwhelming, as there are thousands of people wanting to renew membership at the same time. So how do you get the team involved in improving the membership process? We created a six-week competition and broke the team members into groups of ten, identified by a colour. Even the CEO and the senior managers were involved. The groups competed against each other, being awarded points for a variety of reasons, such as receiving a certificate for excellent guest service from one of our Mystery Shopping staff or if a guest made a positive comment about a team member to a manager. We upped the stakes by including five guest-care managers who would ask team members questions at random times, assessing their knowledge; "Can you tell me what time the raffle is on tonight? Can you tell me what's happening on 26 November?" If they were able to give the correct response, they were awarded points. After the end of the six weeks, points were added up and the winning team was rewarded, both as a team and as individual team members.

TIP

1. Seek input from team members. Ask don't tell.

2. Give feedback. What gets rewarded gets repeated.

3. Make it a game. Add the element of competition to encourage new behaviour.

8. THE CHALLENGE OF BUILDING TEAM LOYALTY

Hospitality venues know about the benefits of rewarding their regular players but don't always pay enough attention to rewarding and recognising their own team members. An anniversary pin is a nice token but not really very practical from the team member's point of view. What team members do like is personal recognition from the CEO in the form of a handwritten note or a conversation to tell them how well they are doing and how management appreciate their efforts. Of course, gifts such as movie tickets or to see a sporting fixture are always appreciated, however, some of our clients have connected with online suppliers who offer the recipient the opportunity to choose a gift of their choice. Here in Australia, we have a company called Red Balloon (www.redballoon.com.au) where you can purchase gift vouchers for memorable experiences. Using a gift voucher as a team member reward let's them choose what they want, shopping for goods as well as experiences such as a fishing trip, sky diving, bridge climb or a romantic dinner.

Having a team loyalty programme behind the scenes is also a good way to reward team members, but it can cross over into a popularity contest and backfire. Many of the venues we work with have looked at this idea, but the perception by many has always been that the managers recognise team members they like rather than rewarding those who are truly deserving of the recognition. You cannot have an effective staff recognition programme that depends solely on a senior manager or duty manager putting forward a team member's name, because there's a good chance that the same people will win over and over again, which is demoralising for the rest of the team. We have seen some team loyalty programmes fail because, after a few months, team members start to lose interest. They say, "Why even bother trying when we are never going to get nominated?" Worse yet, we have seen team members become unwilling participants in the programme because it was blatantly obvious that only the "special ones" were being chosen. So what starts out as a recognition programme turns into a disincentive.

One of our clients has a successful team-member recognition programme in which there are multiple finalists in various categories being recognised by management with smaller gifts and then one team member being selected for Employee of the Year Award for Service and Leadership receiving an educational trip as an incentive. In the past, they have visited trade shows, behind-the-scenes tours at large gaming venues in the USA with senior managers, which are all excellent learning opportunities. Disney also offers some terrific management training programmes, including a backstage look at how Disney's parks work. This is a great incentive, and again, a wonderful educational opportunity for your winning team members. Upon their return, they write a report, give a presentation and share their experience and ideas with their team. The trick is getting the right recognition that works for your venue and having the right management to steer it.

TIP

1. Design an effective team recognition programme.

2. Use educational trips as incentives and team learning experiences.

3. Create a calendar to celebrate team members' birthdays, work anniversaries and special occasions.

9. THE CHALLENGE OF SECURITY AND WELL-BEING OF THE TEAM

Is your venue safe and secure for the team members working there? When the staff leaves at night, is the pathway well lit, and do you offer a security escort?

Putting personal details, full name and photo on staff members' swipe cards presents a security risk. A venue that did this was alerted to this security risk when female team members found they were being stalked.

Promoting mental health in the workplace is everyone's responsibility. At any given time one in five employees is likely to be experiencing a mental health condition. As a VIP manager, you need to take care of yourself, look out for others and know your rights and where to seek help for your team members. There are many organisations that you can connect with that will provide tools and resources for you to implement in the workplace (www. beyondblue.org.au or www.blackdoginstitute.org.au). Smart managers develop an action plan to create a mentally healthy workplace. It's about organisational culture, based on intangible feelings and actions that are difficult to measure: the way people treat each other, loyalty and a sense of camaraderie.

TIP

1. Consider late-night security, especially for female team members.

2. Encourage staff to look after their physical and mental health and check in on how they are feeling.

3. Train staff to prepare and handle challenging situations including armed robbery.

10. THE CHALLENGE OF ROSTERING/SCHEDULING YOUR TEAM

Rostering is a big challenge for management throughout the hospitality industry, whether your team members work full-time, part-time or casually. The difficulty with weekend rostering is that team members usually agree in theory to work a roster when they are hired. Sometimes they have a life event or a party to attend, and the roster winds up being a shift-swapping free for all. Inevitably, you have team members who are always happy to come in when you call at the last moment—until they find out whom they are going to work with, maybe a duty manager they don't like, at which point they say, "No, thanks. I'm washing my hair or rearranging my sock drawer."

In order to be a workplace of choice, your venue must show respect to all of your team members so that when they do come in to work, they work as a strong team. Too often, team members are hired, have a quick induction and then experience their first three or four shifts with three or four different team members, all of whom have their own way of doing things. What we have found over the years is that you can predict a new team member's success by knowing who their initial trainer is. Expert team members are the best trainers. These are people who not only do their jobs well but can also share their skill set and help the new team member through the processes, answer their questions and follow up with them.

New team members experience the opposite when they are trained by someone who shows them how to do the job once and says, "Okay, you are on your own. If you've got any problems, ask me, but think about it first." New team members who are met with this attitude are understandably nervous; they may not have caught on the first time but are reluctant to ask the manager for help because they are scared. They will just keep making the same mistakes over and over until, inevitably, your guest feels the impact of that kind of mistake. That's why correct training from the beginning is so important and needs to be codified.

TIP

1. Know your staff: Undertake a lifestyle survey each year to be aware of any changes in their availability.

2. SMS available shifts to all staff. Whoever responds first is assigned the shift.

3. Plan in advance for busy and quiet seasons. Encourage flexibility with extra shifts and holiday notices.

11. THE CHALLENGE OF ENGAGING YOUR LOCAL COMMUNITY

You can build a loyal base among local community groups, like sporting associations, by sponsoring your local cricket, netball or football club, especially the clubs your team members' children belong to.

Another great way to engage the local community is through socially responsible causes. Many team members may have a second job or other responsibilities. It's not easy to get them together outside the workplace, so try to do your team building within the venue. This group effort can be made around something like Breast Cancer Awareness Month. One of the venues here in Sydney, Australia, went all out with pink ribbons, dyed gloves, sprayed pink grass at their entrance and even pink receipts, raising money for cancer research by holding special morning teas. Other successful efforts involving the larger community have included having team members go together to donate to blood drives.

We have heard many managers say that this kind of group effort really makes an appreciable difference in how people relate to each other in the workplace. Why? Because it makes team members see each other in a new way, as people who have lives beyond the walls of the venue. Not only are they doing something good for the community but they are also learning about each other in a different environment so that when they come back to the workplace, they are a lot more trusting of each other and work more cohesively as a team.

TIP
1. Sponsor and support local sporting clubs, especially those attended by team members or their families.
2. Build your team using socially responsible and charitable events.
3. Publicise, celebrate and share your efforts and achievements.

12. THE CHALLENGE OF BUILDING A GENUINELY CARING AND COMPASSIONATE TEAM

It is important to reward individuals who show initiative, who go above and beyond in their thoughtfulness and guest service. A few years ago, a young team member had finished his shift for the day and, when leaving the venue car park, noticed two elderly ladies trying to battle the bad weather as they walked along the roadway to the venue entrance. He could have simply driven on, but instead, he pulled over, got them into his car, turned around and gave them a ride to the venue front door before heading for home. He never mentioned it to anyone, but the ladies did. When the CEO heard about it, he presented the young man with a special gift at a staff meeting so that he was recognised for his actions of providing superior customer service in front of his peers.

How much do your front-line team members matter to the guest experience? They are everything. From the concierge remembering and greeting guests by name, asking how their night has been and asking about their meal when the guest upon entry said they were dining for the first time. Guests are amazed. In fact, they are WOWED. These team members greet thousands of people, but still they remember specific guests. That's the lasting impression. That's what your guests take home with them as the door shuts behind them, not their interactions with management but that last team member who speaks to them.

Great team members make the effort because they genuinely care. A team member at one of our Sydney venues calls the numbers at Bingo and noticed that an elderly lady who was one of her regulars was missing. She asked around and got the lady's phone number and tried to call her but got no answer. When it came time for the midsession break, she told the folks there that she was going to drive over to the lady's house and check on her, so the break might be a little longer than usual. She found that, indeed, the lady was unwell, and that was why she hadn't come in. She wasn't in any danger, fortunately, but that bingo caller's thoughtfulness and initiative made a huge impression, not just on that one lady but on all the people who were there that night, on the lady's family and on everyone who heard about it. Even the other team members were impressed. The bingo caller had set a benchmark for caring service that made others want to live up to it.

This kind of "above-and-beyond" service may only be possible for smaller venues, those that have that a membership base and that sense of connection between the guests and team members. But training your team members to remember names on member IDs is very important to making that meaningful connection, even in bigger venues.

They should start out formally—Mr. or Mrs. Smith—and only use the first name if and when the guest tells them to. Making this connection through the use of their name makes Venue members in particular feel so much less like a number (or a wallet) and so much more like honoured guests.

TIP
1. Encourage team members to deliver above-and-beyond service.
2. Regularly share examples of great customer experiences delivered by team members.
3. Provide recognition and rewards to team members who perform above and beyond.

CHAPTER 5

Delivering a VIP Experience

The Tim Tam® Moment— Adding More WOWS And Reducing The Ouches

Mantra: Make the most of every guest, every visit, every experience.

WHAT MAKES A TRULY OUTSTANDING EXPERIENCE?

A fabulous *first* impression, a *lasting* memory, help or assistance in a crisis (or *ouch!*), or a moment that makes you say "Wow!" This is known as the FLOW.

Your brain only remembers a few of your many moments and experiences, the few moments that really matter. Typically, these are the earliest and most recent moments. We are conditioned to avoid the painful and seek the pleasurable.

FIRST IMPRESSIONS REALLY COUNT

The sense that something great is about to happen should begin on the way to your venue, with the look of your signage. The car park should offer ease of parking and a pleasant, clean walk to the venue entry. Don't let guests be greeted by a dark and dingy car park and dirty elevators and stairs. Bright lights are welcoming, especially to women arriving alone. Signs should be large and clear, directing guests to where they want to go. Tasteful advertising should draw the eye and be part of the overall décor, even in the car park. Wrap-around posters on columns display upcoming entertainment, create interest and hide ugly concrete; music adds a welcome note, too, and helps your guests to enjoy their long walk when the car park is busy. Think of the Disney experience. If you have been to one of Disney's parks, you know that waiting in line has been turned into part of the entertainment experience. It's even called the preshow, and it's used as an opportunity to entertain and create anticipation.

Turning what could be an irritating wait into your own preshow can be part of your VIP fine dining experience, for instance. When there is a long line at the register to order food, smart venue managers and their chefs take advantage of it to send servers down the queue, offering waiting guests bite-sized samples of first courses. This is a practically no-cost way to not only lower the guests' stress level but tempt them to order the full-size version. When Krispy Kreme first opened in Australia, the company created a thundering demand by simply passing out a free donut to customers waiting in line. By the time customers arrived at the counter, they happily ordered two dozen donuts. The open-design cooking area allowing customers to watch the donuts being made was an interesting concept and, now, many venues have the open-plan kitchen so that guests can see the chefs preparing meals. Guests enjoy seeing the flash of flames as the steak is turned and the swish of the noodles as they roll around the wok. This is the dining entertainment experience.

Lighting design overall has changed considerably in the past few years; venues used to be dark, with no natural light, whereas today guests enjoy views outside and with lighting that is soft and warm. The crystal drop chandeliers and light fittings with pizzazz, even in the restrooms, create an air of luxury and WOW. We are seeing more exotic indoor gardens, bringing the outside in. Green vertical walls look amazing, bringing life to the bar, foyer or walkway. Colour plays a big part, too, in appealing to the eye. Asian guests love to walk over water to enter the gaming areas, particularly if it's a well-stocked pond with colourful koi.

The ambient temperature needs to be right, of course; you don't want guests to shiver, but you don't want them to be over-heated either. It is important that it can be controlled by a couple of degrees either way. Because some gaming machines are so big that you can practically get a tan from standing next to one, the temperature across the whole gaming floor may have to be lowered.

THE VENUE: TAKING YOUR GUESTS WHERE YOU WANT THEM TO GO

Knowing your guests and their preferences and habits is key to getting them where you want them in your venue. Did you know, for example, that in the USA, guests will typically enter and turn to the right, whereas in Australia, they enter and go to the left?

Different guests have different goals. Your High Roller probably wants a straight path to the gaming room. However, other guests want to be immersed immediately in the noise and excitement of your venue. Not only do they want to be greeted by your team members' warm welcome but they also want to hear the gaming machines in the back and the soft music in the lounge.

As they go further into the venue, your guests should be able to see the exciting bars or fine dining venues in the distance. It used to be that as they entered, they were plunged immediately into the gaming machines. Now, it's more of a yellow-brick-road effect of bringing your guest along on a journey. There are a lot of ways to draw your guest along. Some venues do it very well with carpeted "paths" or fancy tiling. Subconsciously, guests follow the path, even though they may not be aware of what management is doing. Paths are also a great directional aid. If you are in a large venue and you ask the staff to direct you to the gaming room or another area, they can say, "See this carpet? Just follow this design all the way and you will get there." Using curved walls can also draw guests in—like a fish trap—to where you want them to go.

You don't want the effect to be vulgar and in-your-face; you want it to be enticing, exciting and stimulating: "Oh, what's that shiny ball over there? I haven't seen that before." Your intelligent, knowledgeable team member is going to give guests the information they need and guide them through. It's not just about telling and pointing. VIP teams take the guest to the area or at least walk the first twenty steps, having a conversation with the guest and highlighting areas of interest as they walk.

GUEST PRIVACY WITHOUT ISOLATION

It is no secret that your guests come to your venue looking for different kinds of experiences: some welcome the social mix and enjoy interacting with the throng, while others are looking for a more private experience. The wise venue managers provide both experiences.

The more serious players want to concentrate on what they are doing and may prefer a sense of privacy, without being entirely isolated. The layout of the gaming room is critical. It must have the correct spacing, correct segmentation of value and correct number of machines in banks that allow the inclusion of all guests, whether they are seeking privacy or want to be right in the middle of the excitement, surrounded by other guests. Partitioning with sheer curtains, scrolled wood panelling, plants or frosted glass provides that sense of privacy.

LASTING IMPRESSIONS: THE TIM TAM® MOMENT—A VIP EXPERIENCE

Guests who come back and tell others about your venue do so because you have given them moments that matter, memorable pleasures and experiences they look forward to repeating.

We often reference what we think of here as the Tim Tam® moment, something that sets your venue apart from the ordinary and from your competition. Tim Tam® biscuits are a product you may not be familiar with if you are not Australian. Simply described, Tim Tams® are filled, chocolate-covered wafers made by Arnott's. The company began with a simple chocolate/chocolate combination and—partnering with a famous Australian pastry chef—expanded into all kinds of exotic flavours, including salted caramel, raspberry with white chocolate and even peanut butter. Between the deliciousness of the product and a clever ad campaign, the biscuits quickly became a national sensation, one that spread globally as people got a taste of them and wanted more. The idea is that you eat them with a cup of tea or coffee: you bite off both ends of the biscuit and suck the beverage through the biscuit. It may sound crass to the uninitiated, but once you have tried it, the Tim Tam® moment will keep you coming back for more.

THE WHOLE NEW LEVEL: WORD OF WEB (WOW)

The explosion of social media—Facebook, Instagram, Pinterest and Twitter—have made the Tim Tam® moment that much more important, because your patrons are taking selfies in your venue or photos of your food and interiors and posting them. This extends the idea of word of mouth to a whole new level, and if the pictures they are posting are appealing, they are, effectively, free advertising. There are some managers who ask guests to comment and rate their meals and facilities through social media and broadcast these posts on large LCD screens throughout the venue to engage and influence other guests' choices.

OVERCOMING THE "OUCH!" FACTOR

Even a wonderfully run venue is going to make some slip-ups in service and have a few disgruntled guests. Everyone makes mistakes; the trick is in recovering from these "Ouch!" experiences and satisfying the guest that you have done your best to make things right. Did you know that "Ouch!" moments are nineteen times more memorable than a pleasurable moment? You can see the importance of making your guests happy again after poor service has turned them off.

CUSTOMER SERVICE RECOVERY (CSR) STRATEGIES
- Apologise, compensate and fix it permanently; make sure it doesn't get repeated.
- Remove your ouches *before* they happen again, whether they concern service, facilities or product. Prompt removal produces the most effective ROI.

- Follow through and follow up. Is your guest satisfied with your attempt at mending your relationship? Make sure you have done the best you can to make it right.
- Social media and reviews can hurt, but don't be tempted to respond in kind to an unpleasant review. Instead, write a thoughtful response that includes a reiteration of your apology and details your attempts to make things right, as well as your intention to be certain that no guest will ever have a similar unpleasant experience in your venue.

THE WOW EXPERIENCE

There's one thing your guests all share: the hunger for the WOW experience that takes their breath away. The WOW experience is what sends them home saying, "Oh, my goodness, did you see this?" or "Have you been there?" or "You have got to try this" or "You have got to see what they offer."

In creating your WOW, you want to touch all five senses. One smart venue, years before any other venue did the same here in Australia, spearheaded the look and offering in venues. It went from just being focused on gaming machines and beverages to creating the culture of a five-star hotel. From the moment you stepped out of your car, the environment was designed to present a different look, a different scent, with different music. As you walked throughout the venue, the smell, the look and the lighting changed in each area. It was a very creative way to break up the interior of the venue without using walls and made it a series of unique and specific experiences. This VIP level of care extended even to the ladies' room, where the first thing guests saw was a lavish bouquet of orchids. There was lovely scented soap and hand lotion. Spotless white hand towels were rolled up in pretty baskets at each sink. The taps were touchless, as were the toilets.

Restrooms may seem unimportant, but if you walk into a neglected, dirty or just dingy restroom, the impression you get is that management doesn't really care about you, and whatever impression you had of luxury beyond the restrooms is quickly lost. Some venues even have mini-televisions in each cubicle—again, for that WOW factor. In the men's room, one venue installed one-way glass so that the men standing at the urinals can look out and watch the gaming machines. Even the porcelain bowls have blowflies painted on them to correct the aim. These may seem like gimmicks, but they get people talking about that venue. Soft music, marble or other luxury finishes and gold-plated taps—all of these special touches add to the effect of luxury you are trying to achieve and bring the WOW your guest craves.

Of course, that WOW factor needs to be present in every area of the venue, starting with what you see before you even come in. Some venues have features outside the entrance to attract a crowd: themed shows, sound and light shows, holographics and even erupting volcanoes.

The key to getting the most out of providing a VIP experience to people outside your venue is getting them to come inside, so the welcome must be memorable, with smiling and knowledgeable door people to greet incoming guests. Some venues have a team member acting more as a concierge who can wave you to the left or right when you enter and ask for directions. Again, that's the heart of the WOW experience: making your guests feel valued and special, as though they are stepping up to a luxury-level experience.

Here are some ideas that other venues use effectively to broaden their offerings and provide another source of fun and income:

1. Provide space for entrepreneurs who don't want to sit in their home office. This is an ideal way for business people to connect, and it opens the doors to another group of guests at your venue. Add some comfortable lounges with comfortable chairs and low tables as well as one or two communal tables. Provide free Wi-Fi close to the bar and food or in a coffee shop on the premises. They need space to work, but these business people still want to be a part of the action.

2. The selfie craze is likely to continue as long as we have mobile phones, so why not create a backdrop in your venue where guests can take a selfie or be with friends? It could be a mountain scene, beach or the latest set of a movie or favourite television show. Make sure your logo is strategically placed on the wall. Have the guests share posts on their favourite social media.

3. Guests want to know what your team does for the community, so take a video of the next charity BBQ with your team dressed in their venue-branded T-shirts, cooking the sausages and interacting with people. The team could manage the BBQ at a blood donation event, a run for cancer or some other charitable fund-raiser.

For more tips and ideas go to our website at http://thevipp.com

THE VIP DINING EXPERIENCE

Your food really has to WOW your guests. Over the past decade, what draws guests to a venue has become "all about the food". Food has become a major draw card, if not *the* major draw card, for venue selection. Take a look at the crockery you use. Is it commercial-style crockery or elegant and special? When venues change from standard heavy-duty crockery to an oval plate, a square plate or even to fine china, it makes such a difference to your guests. And don't have your servers carry massive trays of food. Again, that is not a VIP experience.

There's also the "shabby chic" approach, especially in the less formal coffee shop, where colour has taken on a bigger role in décor and accoutrements. The crockery is all different colours to make it look more modern and edgy. And if you are still plating slices of plastic-wrapped cake in a glass case, please don't. Display the whole cake on a rotating plate with great lighting like a Hollywood production. If you are concerned about wastage, only display four pieces of each cake or slice at a time and have the rest in the fridge, then replenish as needed. The display is still abundant with offerings but it is not plastic wrapped within an inch of it's life. Use coloured plates, wooden mini-trays angled to display tasty sweet slices and healthy treats, jars of cookies complemented with a variety of coffees, selected green teas and more. Again, you want that WOW factor that draws guests in.

FOOD AND BEVERAGES THAT ATTRACT WOWS

When it comes to food and beverages, every detail counts: impressive food displays, descriptive signage, ice displays, beer taps—everything down to the cutlery. It is also important that the décor complements your food offerings.

Pop-up food stations are increasingly popular inside and outside venues, because they create a fun space for people to take a quick break and grab a coffee or a snack in a hurry if they don't want to wait for a seat in the restaurant. For example, one venue has a little donut cart passing out free donuts to guests in the gaming area, which serves to draw people in and keep them there.

DRAGON TIP

The luxury experience in dining is particularly important to your Asian clientele, who appreciate the finer finishes, china and service. Again, check the Feng Shui of your layout and make sure you are not making obvious errors.

Keeping that WOW experience going requires increasingly frequent updates and redos. Whereas you might have redecorated areas every five years in the past, now you probably have to refresh the décor every two or three years. Decorator trends are always changing, and soft refurbishment has become more common. But even small changes can refresh a space. New paint and scattered rugs and cushions create a quick and relatively cost-effective new look.

It is the feeling of WOW you want your guests to have when they come to your venue; it's the differentiating factor that makes them willing to get dressed, leave their comfortable sofas and come to your venue. When they get there, not only do they have their expectations met because of what you offer them but you go above and beyond.

Giving your guests their big dose of WOW from the moment they approach your venue and extending it to every experience they have while they are there will make them your loyal guests. What they tell their friends about that experience via social media will extend the reach of your WOW factor and provide great word-of-mouth advertising you can't buy. For the latest tips and ideas on décor and food and beverage trends go to http://thevipp. com

VIP Advocacy

The Three Steps To Guest Commitment—Going Beyond Vip Experiences And Guest Loyalty

Mantra: VIP advocacy is earned by building
relationships, reputation and trust.

So how do you get your guests to consistently come back to your
venue and tell others about their experience?

Essentially, creating loyal VIP guests is a three-step journey:

1. Deliver a *VIP Guest Experience*: exceed your guests'
   expectations.

2. Encourage *Guest Loyalty*: nurture your guest to increase
   visitation and spend.

3. Develop *Guest Advocacy*: transform your guests into
   advocates for your venue.

To succeed at all three steps of the journey, you have to deliver that
WOW experience each and every time. Your most loyal VIPs will
have the highest expectations of you. You've delivered a WOW
moment to them before, so if they feel your venue is losing its

lustre or your team's service is dropping off, you will hear about it from them. In this chapter, we're going to talk about the different ways in which you can make that romance last and move your semi-committed regulars to the loyal-guest category by going above and beyond the level of service they expect in order to make them feel genuinely valued.

STEP 1: VIP GUEST EXPERIENCE

Show your guests they are valued

The first thing that makes guests feel valued is, simply, recognition. In an increasingly impersonal world, a genuine smile and a greeting using the guest's name are two invaluable ways to make a connection. If your front-line team regularly looks at members' cards, they should make such connections and develop a positive rapport.

Doing the little things makes all the difference. One particular venue in Sydney shows, through its helpful and caring staff, that all guests are valued. If a guest looks a little lost while walking around the venue, the team member will take the initiative to come up and say, "May I help you? You look a bit lost."

But why wait for someone to need help? Any sort of kind, informal interaction with guests goes a long way. For example, team members may say, "Oh, gee, it's hot today" or "You look like you need a coffee." If your team recognises that a guest is from out of town, they may make a connection by saying, "I've got family members who live there" or "I've been there on a holiday." That makes the critical first impression. If the guests are on holiday, they may decide to become members now to save money down the road if they intend to come back again and again.

Our Mystery Shopping staff are always impressed when a team member takes the time to tell them about the benefits the venue offers. When you've completed renovations, for example, your team might suggest to guests that they check out what's new. This shows a sense of pride and gives the invitation that personal touch when it's done in a conversation.

MAKING YOUR GUESTS FEEL WELCOME AND SPECIAL

Now let's face it: not all of your team members are going to be equally gifted when it comes to developing a connection with your guests. You can't teach attitude; you can only teach skills. Some team members have those wonderful personalities that allow them to make friends with everybody, and those people should be your front-line representatives. No matter how old your guests are, everything rides on making that connection and making them feel they are valued, VIP guests. They should feel they are more than just another person coming through the door. Every connection is a potential success story, whether your team greets a familiar guest and casually asks about their recent operation, or they offer a cheerful greeting instead of a cool reception to an imposing male guest who, at first glance, looks like trouble. It begins by setting the right tone at the front door and continuing that VIP level of service throughout the visit. If your team sees someone struggling to carry their tray back to the table, for instance, they should cheerfully help them without waiting to be asked. The best teams know their regular guests well enough to help them before they even pick up the tray.

And don't forget how helpful national flags on staffs' ID badges or lapels can be to make your foreign guests feel welcome.

Those whose mother tongue is not English are relieved when they see someone identified as able to speak their language.

EMPOWER YOUR FRONT LINE TO GO ABOVE AND BEYOND

Your team needs to be empowered to bend the venue rules when it comes to going above and beyond in service. One of our Mystery Shoppers had a broken leg. While she was playing a gaming machine, she asked a team member to bring her a Coke. The team member said, at first, "Oh, we don't do tray service." Then she saw that her leg was in a cast and immediately said, "Sorry. I didn't see your cast. Don't worry. I'll go and get it for you."

There are so many great ways to help your front line add value by making the right choices, from hiring the right people to rewarding and recognising staff who consistently surpass normal operating procedure for the guests' benefit. Everyone on the team, from the doorman to the CEO, has to strive for this gold standard of service to build a culture of excellence that will earn your venue and your brand loyal, committed and satisfied guests.

EXTENDING THE LOYALTY

Building a VIP experience goes beyond the guests focused on a night at the gaming machines or the card tables: you should be going out of your way to offer significant others and families a wonderful experience, too. Providing a diversified experience is a trend that started in Las Vegas, but it has quickly caught on internationally.

Health and wellness has caught on worldwide: day spas, gyms and fitness classes are popular with a wide range of guests. Laser tag, bowling and kids' play equipment let prospective guests know that you run a venue where everyone can have fun. Providing fun, safe, supervised activities for kids; tasty, health-conscious foods on a kids' menu; and options to eat at an outside area instead of just a bar can go a long way to promoting a family-friendly atmosphere that enhances your brand. If you have a smokers' area, remember that it doesn't have to be dingy and unhealthy. Smokers often have non-smoking friends and family with them, so make sure that the smoking areas are well ventilated and well lit. Well-landscaped outdoor areas are a great option that allows everyone to have a good time together.

THREE TIPS IN DELIVERING A VIP GUEST EXPERIENCE

1. Make your guest feel special.
2. Empower your team with knowledge and confidence to promote your venue's benefits.
3. Encourage the use of the membership card by having all team members ask for it at every transaction.

STEP 2: GUEST LOYALTY

Valuing your guests' loyalty

Many venues hand out incentives to new loyalty programme members. For example, if there is a gym on the premises, guests may receive a free casual visit. Naturally, when they get there, they are given a full tour and a personal fitness assessment. If this is done right, they will join up there and then.

When tiered loyalty programmes were first introduced, venue managers got very excited about this new type of programme's potential to increase player spending, provide more information about their guests, and offer the opportunity to reward guests' various "spend" levels. Guests were intrigued and quickly became members because persuasive advertising was very effective in selling them the dream that they would build a great wealth of points—that is, until they read the fine print or discovered from asking staff that the ratio of points-to-dollar-spend was tilted very much in favour of the venue. Many of our client venues that introduced a loyalty system, however, did not have the staff to monitor the programme, and when their members discovered the low points-to-dollar-spend ratio, a number of venues shelved the programme.

More recently, major changes have been made to loyalty programme levels. Better point allocation is now offered, including gifts to "surprise and delight" and recognition of High Rollers through VIP hosts who look after High Rollers and understand their needs.

If you want your guests to be loyal to you, you must be loyal to them. Many venues reward members who play the machines— no matter their membership level—with free soft drinks and hot beverages when they insert their membership card into the machine. In this way, all members are thanked for their loyalty and those who choose to spend more at the venue are rewarded in a more substantial manner.

MAKING IT EASIER TO BECOME A MEMBER

Recently, one of our long-standing clients successfully introduced a tiered loyalty programme for the very first time in their venue. The venue's revenue grew by an astonishing 17% in the first three months and players who had not visited for a long time returned on a regular playing schedule. The loyalty programme wasn't groundbreaking; other venues had done it before, but it was new to the guests who loved that venue. It is their venue of choice and now that they are being rewarded for their loyalty, and they share their approval with their friends and coworkers.

The programme is building brand advocates. What is important is that the venue management continues to offer achievable and interesting benefits to each membership tier to maintain loyalty after the honeymoon period has worn off.

It has to be easy, and it has to be quick. If there is one thing that prospective members dislike, it is queuing to join, especially when there is nothing to entertain them as they wait. From a management perspective, the time wasted standing in a queue could be better spent in the venue, using the venue's facilities. A simple way to solve the problem is by implementing an express membership registration that speeds up the process and eliminates the lines entirely. Your prospective members can pick up membership forms wherever they happen to be: at the bar, at a restaurant, even in the gaming room. They fill the form out and give it to a team member who puts it into the express box, similar to those boxes hotels use for express checkouts. The forms are taken to the membership team, who enter the new members' details into the system, and at some stage during their visit, the new members swing by reception to pick up their membership card. Alternatively, the forms are hand-delivered by a staff member, and new loyalty programme members don't even have to pick up their membership card themselves. In some countries, new members have their photo taken. All the team member has to do is verify the prospective loyalty programme members' identity through their driver's licence, take down those details and make sure the prospective member signs the back of the card—and the new members are all set! If there is a fee for membership (as there is in Australia), management must come up with a solution that keeps the guests enjoying themselves instead of standing in a queue.

Again, the team members' support of this programme is crucial to your loyalty system paying off. They've got to be diligent and helpful in reminding guests to use their cards at every transaction, including inserting the card into the gaming machine.

DIFFERENTIATING YOUR MEMBERSHIP TIERS

Venues mark their cards in various ways to indicate the tiered loyalty programme. The levels may be differentiated by colour, gem stones or other insignia. Each venue sets its scale of points earned relative to money spent, but to become card-using members, prospective members have to clearly see the benefits to them.

Some guests avoid using their cards at all. Some get self-conscious and want to remain anonymous, while others don't see the value in passing the card over when they make a purchase or inserting it into the gaming machine. Some don't want anyone to be able to track their spending and play pattern. For various reasons, not every venue has a tiered loyalty programme. Instead, some venues give higher returns to guests playing the machines.

Another big concern that guests often mention about loyalty programmes is the feeling of being judged by the colour of their card. It bears repeating that just treating guests according to the colour of their card is not acceptable because it can inhibit guests' loyalty or make them uncomfortable and unwilling to move through your tiered loyalty programme. A number of venues looked at this problem and decided they would have a loyalty programme but would treat all their members the same. The tiered part of the programme has to be above and beyond the standard, which may include, for example, giving *everybody* a free soft drink or tea or coffee at the machine.

Some venue managers call it an awards programme, not a loyalty programme, and guests respond more favourably to that description. Whether it's a differentiation in words or their own mindset, the team members believe they are rewarding all of the guests, and guests see great value in it. For instance, in Australia, we can pay our utility and telephone bills by using points, which many people perceive as an added value.

A common issue with tiered loyalty programmes is when and how the venue decides where the guests are on the tiers. You may have experienced this with an airline loyalty programme if you fly often: in September you feel you're just a couple of points away from getting to platinum, but then October comes around and you're back to zero again. The same thing can happen with venues' tiered loyalty programmes: points are cleared out every year, leaving members to start the new year at zero again. Therefore, it is important that your guests see the value in the programme and have the opportunity to spend on items that are not ridiculously inflated in value and are something they need or want. For example, some venues partner with stores offering quality merchandise that can be purchased with the venue points. Some venue guests can pay their household utility bills with their venue points, or they can buy entertainment tickets, food or bar drinks with their points. One of our clients held a very successful white goods sale one year and filled a function room in their venue with a range of washing machines, ovens and other white goods that members could purchase with their points.

The key to tiered loyalty programmes is maintenance and monitoring. Smart venue managers employ dedicated team members who carefully monitor member spending to ascertain members' tiered loyalty level on a monthly, bi-monthly or quarterly basis. The decision comes down to the venue. However, the most common is bi-monthly monitoring to move members up a level and twice yearly monitoring to move members down a level.

USING YOUR TEAM MEMBERS TO PROMOTE LOYALTY BENEFITS

When guests become members, they are given flyers that tell them all about the loyalty programme. Many fold these flyers and place them in their pockets, and they may never be looked at again before going through the wash. For that reason it's critical that the venue team members are knowledgeable and promote the programme to new members, advising them on their entitlements. It's the only way to run a successful loyalty programme. A proactive team that asks questions of new members to ascertain their interests provides an opening to a conversation by highlighting what the venue offers. For example, a new member may say she competes in charity running races. The team member could then tell the new guest member about the gym, personal trainers and the great class schedule that takes place from 5.30 a.m. till 10 p.m. each day.

One of our venues here offers a free valet service to its High Rollers, but no matter how much they advertise this offer or how many promotional flyers they hand out, the High Rollers never seem to know about it. That's why the success of programmes like this comes down to the VIP gaming hosts saying to guests, as they greet them, "Did you drive here? Did you remember to use our valet service?" The VIP gaming host may have to remind guests several times before they remember to use the valet service, but eventually they will.

To get guests excited about using their cards and being a part of a rewards system, you have to offer quality gifts. Some venues have a dedicated loyalty shop; others have a number of display cabinets. However, items that are not displayed and merchandised well do not encourage guests to spend their points and use their cards.

What are you offering in return for points? Can points be exchanged for a free gym membership? Can members get vouchers that can be spent at the local grocery store, for instance? Some venues provide vouchers that can be used at local retailers. The big advantage of this kind of exchange is that, in some cases, the venue can triple its database when members are told they can use their points at X appliance store, and X appliance store tells prospective members they can earn points at the venue that they can spend in the appliance store. Thus each business feeds off the other's database of guests/customers who might not otherwise have overlapped at all.

You can take tips from the excellent loyalty programmes run by other kinds of businesses, too. When you use your grocery chain rewards card at the store, you may not get anything off the price directly, but you could get a discount on petrol and points that go toward your airline rewards programme, as the two programs are linked. During one Christmas holiday period, the two major supermarket chains in Australia sent a coupon book to their members to use in addition to their cards, at each purchase, to gain more points and discounts. What additional benefit can you offer your members, at special times of the year, that would motivate them to come into your venue more often?

The whole concept of loyalty programmes is an offshoot of the old-fashion incentive/discount coupon books offered by local merchants—for instance, $5 off a haircut, $4 off meat at the butcher's. It was a very basic programme and was chiefly intended to tempt new customers into trying out the participating businesses. These incentive/discount coupons programmes developed into loyalty card programmes. The cards would be stamped or clipped at each purchase until customers reached a certain number of purchases, for which they were rewarded. For instance, if customers bought six items, they could get a seventh item of equal or lesser value at no charge.

Whenever we present a front-line training programme, we ask the participants which membership programmes they belong to. Most of the time, they tell us they're not members of anything. When we ask them to go through their wallets or purses, they're surprised at how many membership cards they actually have. They don't recognise the value of the membership or loyalty programmes, because they're so conditioned to just handing over their cards without any comment form the person handling the card and their money. Most of the time, they don't even know what they are being rewarded with. Maybe, at the end of the year, they get a $5 voucher, but meanwhile the business is gathering quite a bit of information on them and filling their inbox with unsolicited emails that are irrelevant.

The programmes have gone from their local roots to having international reach. Now, anyone who travels regularly collects hotel rewards, car rental rewards and so on, as well as air miles or perks. It doesn't matter where you are. With multinational companies you can receive rewards/offers from around the world.

The cross-pollination of clients' loyalty to venues within the same company/group is also offering more and more options. Some venues may even consider building a relationship with other venues in another state or overseas, where they can agree upon a "swap" of High Rollers as a "surprise and delight" gift. There will always be those who worry about losing their High Rollers this way, but our feeling is that they're more likely to return even more committed than before, because you have given them this great experience. They may be travelling anyway. So why not be the venue they thank for their "surprise-and-delight" gift? They will certainly tell other High Rollers, which may, in turn, increase their spend in your venue.

ENCOURAGE THE USE OF MEMBER CARDS

As technology improves, so does loyalty programme identification design. The problem with cards or coupons is that most guests will forget to present them and miss out on discounts and points. The venue team needs to ask for the card at every transaction to inform members about how much they have saved and how many points they have gained. Doing this reminds those members who have forgotten their card, and guests who haven't yet become members, of what they are missing. It will not take long for them to start remembering to bring and use their cards. It's the instant savings—this instant gratification—that makes guests feel good and glad they are members.

Inevitably, there will be players who don't want to put their cards into the machines for whatever reasons. We've seen this particularly in Macau, where as few as 5% of the players use cards. In Australia, if you're getting between 40 and 60% of your players to use their cards, you're at about the average. If you're only getting 20%, you need to have a hard look at your rewards system, because your guests are telling you it's not appealing. Having to spend $1,000 to earn a hot dog is not much of an incentive!

MEMBERSHIP OFFERS

Some venues sweeten their offer with a free coffee and cake at the coffee shop, which is a great way to get guests in there and looking at what else the venue has to offer. Sometimes it's a two-for-one at the bistro, or it could be $5 worth of free raffle tickets. At other venues it could be a free visit to the Health Club or raffle tickets.

Three tips to encourage guest loyalty:

1. Focus on quality to Surprise and Delight.

2. Implement Express Membership, which is efficient, not rushed.

3. Create tiers of interest and value.

STEP 3: GUEST ADVOCACY

Guest commitment

Whether your venue offers a loyalty programme or not, guest commitment is something you need to earn, every day and in every interaction. Like any other relationship, the moment you take it for granted, it's likely to disappear. Make sure that "guests first" is the mantra that you and everyone who works for you keep foremost in their minds.

Smart managers are always thinking out of the square to provide their guests with a new experience or a WOW moment.

Smart venue managers analyse trends in the market place and have a clear understanding of what appeals to their market. Being one step ahead in what you offer your guests and personalising it, makes them feel special and is the key to advocacy. Sometimes it's just the little things that make the biggest difference. For instance, when guests enter their room at a resort, a personal hand-written note wishing them a great stay (using their name) can make that WOW impact, or the WOW difference can be a front-line team member who remembers the guests' names or where they are from if they're on holiday, after meeting them only once.

THREE TIPS TO DEVELOP GUEST ADVOCACY:
1. Involve chosen guests in the selection of furnishings and furniture for the venue.
2. Highlight members' achievements and awards in sport, dance, education,

community and so on. Feature Venue Ambassadors in your venue magazine or on your social media channel

3. Appoint members to assist in organising event days for charity and supplying the venue team with T-shirts, pins, water bottles and so on, marked with your venue brand, along with flyers.

CHAPTER 7

Attracting More VIPs

Drawing A Crowd With Entertainment, Dining And Décor

Mantra: Different things attract different
guests at different times.

Let's look further at entertainment, dining and décor. These three aspects of your venue can attract prospective guests and wow them or have them running for the exits. They set the tone for the level of experience your guests will have. Neglecting them limits your guest numbers, no matter how amazing your restrooms are.

ACTS THAT ATTRACT

Those of you who have been to Las Vegas know how much glamour and excitement headline entertainment brings to the experience of gaming there. This has been true since its founding days, when the Rat Pack and their associates had their names splashed all over the marquees. However, the trend is moving toward having young and new entertainers who are rising stars or are on their way to fame and fortune. The idea is that instead of entertainers

101

going there at the end of their career, they go there as part of their journey.

Smaller venues may offer old-time acts from the seventies, eighties and nineties. However, these entertainers are getting older and may not be performing at their best, and young people won't come out to see that sort of act. So how do you best showcase entertainment that appeals to the young and the young at heart?

Some venues are moving toward putting shows on earlier in a private room so that the older guests can have an early dinner, see the show, spend some time in the gaming room and get on their way. Later, you bring on the entertainment that appeals to your younger guests. Having different programming for different age groups is key to getting them in, and it's got to be on their schedule.

IS THERE MORE THAN GAMING MACHINES? DEFINITELY

Many venues offer low-value games such as keno, bingo, housie and hoy. Some venue managers complain about the bingo games, but we have often said that we'd rather see fifty people filling seats than see fifty empty seats. Promotions at machines are popular. For instance, if a guest has a $2 win, they put their hand up and are given a card that allows them to enter a raffle. Entertainment draws a lot of members, and the numbers go up every week. Venues that have membership cards all have a swipe machine at the venue entrance. When members swipe their cards, they may be given raffle tickets or a free coffee in the coffee shop. Raffles are big in some venues and can include toy raffles, meat raffles and even seafood raffles.

The majority of venues now have free Wi-Fi. You come into the coffee shop, you buy a cake and a drink and you get the password and that allows you free Wi-Fi for an hour. After that hour, you will have to buy something else to get a refreshed password.

Outdoor jazz band concerts on Sunday afternoons are a big hit in summer. Some venues keep the party going after dark with a DJ. Even the small venues may have a pianist in the lounge, which can make the venue the place to be.

Lawn bowls is seen by many as an old person's game, and bowls venues are usually small with dated décor. Many venues with dwindling membership are being forced to close their doors. However, there are some smart managers who have created these amazing little venues that are popular with the younger generations. They offer fun and team competition with barefoot bowls, a very popular game on warm, summer, weekend afternoons. When teamed with great cuisine, offering an original taste and perhaps using just local produce, these venues have changed the vibe of what was, once, an almost-deserted venue used only by older members and struggling to keep the doors open.

DRAGON TIP

A big favourite with Asian guests is mah-jong. It is a great attraction and an adjunct to gaming, and if you are serving that demographic, you should offer that, too.

If your local area has an Asian demographic, consider providing what these guests want in the way of entertainment. Karaoke is always a winner, as are bands appealing to different cultural groups, and many places have special lounges that offer just that. Multicultural offerings will bring new people to your venue, and of course, the bands themselves bring their own fan base out, which gives you the opportunity to wow them and create new regular guests from that one visit. People who come initially for the entertainment almost always wind up playing the machines or the tables as well, whereas those who come solely for the buffet, for instance, tend to eat and leave without visiting the gaming areas.

Some venues have isolated their dining areas in a way that puts them on a straight line to and from the front door. This increases the exit rate and decreases spend in the venue. Where the floor plan permits, smart venue managers create a pathway that takes exiting diners past the gaming area, the coffee shop with a lounge area and even entertainment, all of which may tempt them to stay a little longer. The smell of freshly brewed coffee and an attractive display of cakes is hard to pass by!

And whatever you do, don't choose entertainment strictly according to your own preferences. You may love country and Western or even punk rock. However, who are your demographic? They are the ones sitting in your venue and spending. Some guests are happy with background music. Others are there to watch, listen and be a part of the entertainment. Whether the entertainment is in the open lounge area or in a separate room, the offering has to fit with the demographic. You have to attract the demographic you want. Where the entertainment is located can affect the guests and their desire to stay longer. Venue gaming analysis has shown a correlation with longer and stronger player spend when entertainment is offered because guests enjoy it and therefore stay longer and spend more.

THE DINING EXPERIENCE

Food trends are being driven by guests who want to enjoy quality food products and a variety of cuisines with interesting menus that change seasonally and have tempting specials. The buffet is still with us, and in some venues the quality is high. But many diners have moved away from this option. However, you need to show sensitivity to the preferences of your guests.

Growth lies in the tapas menu, which is increasingly popular with those who like the small plates idea, usually served with an ethnic flavour. The sharing experience is what makes it special, and guests, by and large, are willing to overlook the added expense in exchange for the fun, social aspect.

Themed restaurants featuring elaborate, almost theatrical décor are increasingly popular. Think Rainforest Café or a themed Italian café complete with cobble stones, moped and even laundry hanging from washing lines, as though you were dining in a little back street in Rome. A railway theme, for instance, with train carriages and memorabilia can appeal to adults and children alike.

THE DÉCOR EXPERIENCE

Over the years, trends in dining décor have gone from white linen restaurants to casual settings, and trends change continually. Dining décor is driven not just by fashion trends but also by your demographic. Guests from Asia appreciate having their cuisine prepared in their own style rather than being offered only Western food. They want to be seated in a restaurant that uses white linen and is decorated with red and gold furnishings and accessories.

They may want to live that Western lifestyle when they are on holiday, but they still want to be able to eat their own food and in luxurious surroundings.

The pop-up or instant restaurant is a great way to surprise and delight your guests and is more cost effective than a complete restaurant makeover. These food offerings complement and expand your existing dining options. The pop-up restaurant has become a favourite at venues worldwide over the last year or so. It might be a coffee stand with little edible treats, or it could be something even more specialised—for instance, a pop-up place that only serves duck, fish or pork. Many of them make the dining experience more immersive by having food prepared in front of the diners. This idea began when architects created open-plan kitchens and dining areas that flowed. However, this type of layout necessitates retraining chefs and other kitchen team members to be hyper-aware of cleanliness and how they work with the food, since they are now onstage, not behind the scenes. A good chef mixes a salad with bare hands, but your diners don't want to see that. When open kitchens premiered, venues were bombarded with complaints about dirty aprons, food handled with bare hands and people shouting at each other. One venue even trained a camera on the chefs making pizzas. The video was shown on the LCD screens out in the restaurant, which might sound like fun to watch, but it drew complaints about the chef scratching his nose and touching his hair.

Before cooking shows became popular on TV, guests were wowed by this type of showmanship. They have become a little bit desensitised because every night of the week another cooking show appears with somebody else demonstrating how easy it is to cook a gourmet meal in 30 minutes after a long day at work! In fact, we'd venture to say that cooking shows generally have turned everyone into an expert restaurant critic.

THE WOW DINING FACTOR

The finer points of food presentation are increasingly important to this newly critical audience, whether it's in your restaurant or function centre. You can have an amazing chef, but if the food is not presented well on the plate, and if the person who puts that plate down isn't smiling and wishing guests a good evening, and if the cutlery has yesterday's hard, encrusted egg on it, it doesn't matter how great that meal was when it left the kitchen. The guests won't enjoy it at all. Yes, the food must be excellent, but there are a number of steps to take regarding how diners want it placed in front of them.

In the past the WOW experience meant having the waiter arrive at your table with your meal placed under a posh silver cover. After you finished your meal, the waiter presented you with a cleansing sorbet while sweeping away the crumbs with a miniature broom and pan. It was all very theatrical. Now, it's the food itself that has to provide the spectacle.

Food consciousness has exploded, particularly in the area of international cuisine. People love to have the chance to sample cuisines to which they might not previously have been exposed. Providing them with that opportunity gives them another reason to come to your venue. People care about quality and are prepared to pay more for a well-prepared, interesting meal. Some guests complain about food prices in venues, yet would be happy to pay more at a restaurant down the road. Somehow they believe that because it is a gaming venue, the costs should be subsidised.

However, if you give them high-quality food consistently, they will accept paying the higher price for quality.

Experimentation with exotic menus obviously comes with some risk. Some venues have added rabbit and even goat to their menus. The goat might be successful but not the rabbit depending on the demographic of their guests. Experimenting is great, but first take a look at your target market. However, diners don't want to settle for a boring meat pie and chips, either.

Food is like fashion; it comes in cycles, sometimes bringing back old things like fondue, which has been recently rediscovered. Done right, fondue looks spectacular coming out to the table, which raises its WOW quotient.

For more food trends and ideas, visit http://thevipp.com.

BEVERAGE CHOICES THAT COMPLEMENT YOUR FOOD

Guests have become choosier about what they want to drink, too, so your beverages have to be served with WOW—and that includes beer. Years ago, it was just a handful of beers on tap or in bottles, familiar brands, nothing too fancy. But now, with the influx of craft beers and boutique brands, people are looking for something new and intriguing, and beer tasting is challenging wine tasting as a pastime and a passionate interest.

Microbreweries have emerged all over Australia and the USA. And even the bigger beer producers are getting into it, buying up small craft breweries to produce beer under boutique labels. Some venues are experimenting with new beer offerings by buying a case to see if their guests like it and promoting a different one each week. Guests are asked to fill out a tasting score sheet as they would at a wine tasting, and whichever beer has been the top scorer that month gets added to the permanent menu.

Moving up in popularity is old-fashioned cider, in its new, crafted, flavoured iteration. Younger drinkers dismissed it for years, but now it's resurging in popularity and is especially big in university pubs. International beers now stand alongside locally brewed beers in fridges at venue bars and are even paired with meals in restaurants. The humble beer is no longer a beverage to be chugged but to be enjoyed and savoured in an ice-cold glass.

The WOW factor of wines has increased, as guests have become more sophisticated in their preferences. Wine has always been popular, of course, but increasingly, a lot of the venue restaurants will suggest fine wine pairings on their menus—even at the bistro—as you'd see at a high-end restaurant. People appreciate the suggestion and are more likely to experiment if they have some guidance. Wine-of-the-Month is a big thing, too, encouraging customers to try something new by the bottle or the glass. Wines from overseas are showing up on more menus, including more selections from large and boutique blends from wineries all around the world.

WINE KNOWLEDGE

Not every venue can employ a sommelier. However, all team members in the dining and bar areas should have basic knowledge of the beverage products on offer. A feature of your venue can be a wall of wine that displays rows of bottles. The sommelier can show the bottles to guests and talk about their relative merits. Of course, this kind of thing works best where your guests are more likely to go for higher-end dining. But you will find many guests are willing to spend a little more for a special glass of a higher-quality wine, especially when it's to accompany a pricier meal. Obviously, for guests with less discerning palates, you want to have red and white house wines of decent quality, but you must be ready to appeal to your upscale guests, too. Don't be too quick to dismiss the idea that your regular guests won't go for it or that they are too lowbrow to care. You may judge people by where they live, but these people will pay $7 to $10 for a nice glass of wine because they know that it works well with their meal.

Smart managers have introduced private VIP rooms for VIP guests to gather and entertain a small group of friends. A small private room close to the bar area that is lavishly decorated with a couple of comfortable lounges, low tables, soft lighting and a team member who is the room host. These styles of rooms are particularly appealing to guests from an Asian culture. These rooms could also be used as private tasting rooms for wines as a surprise and delight gift to your High Rollers.

COCKTAIL DELIGHTS!

The younger female guests have more disposable income and are prepared to pay a higher price for a cocktail than perhaps their mothers—because they are still living at home! Happy hours offering cocktails at reduced prices or a cocktail of the week or month are very popular. A good bartender or cocktail waiter can dress a glass as a good chef dresses a plate, making it look really attractive and appealing.

When you put together your beverage menu, don't skimp on length and description, especially when it comes to craft beers, fine wines, and fancy cocktails. Use descriptive words and phrases that sell. People really like to read about what they are going to order, and some of the wine and beverage menus at our finer venues run six or more pages long. Look at funky ways to present your beverage list—mini-clipboards or chalkboards, for instance.

DRAGON TIP

The Asian market's interest in fine wines, especially reds, is increasing. Asians are very interested in learning about wines, and your Asian High Rollers are likely to appreciate special "perks" like wine connoisseur courses.

THE ART OF TEA AND THE RISE OF THE BARISTA COFFEE SERVICE

Smart venue management offer tray service to players at the gaming machines, with soft drinks being free. They also offer the milky specialty teas that are so loved by their Asian guests. In some venues they have made tea pouring a true art form. The tea comes on a special wooden tray, and the server pours the tea in the traditional manner, explaining the various parts of the ritual. The venue offers multiple blends, including the beautiful flower tea which, when infused in hot water, literally blooms before your eyes in its glass pot. This attention to detail really brings the WOW to what could otherwise be just a cup of tea, and it gives your guests something to tell their friends about.

Barista coffee made and served in the gaming room in place of the self-serve coffee machine is a concept that is catching on due to guests' requests. When venues have their supplier create a special blend of Arabica or Robusta coffee types, it takes the guest to a whole new experience level.

FOOD TO GO

An intriguing new trend is food that guests can take away. In the case of one venue here in Australia they introduced an artisan bakery, at first, the bakery supplied only the venue. However, the baked goods quickly became so popular that the bakery now sells its products at local markets. This gives the venue an opportunity to tap into a local monthly market that it would otherwise probably not have had access to, because if market shoppers want to buy more of the artisan bakery's goods before the next monthly market, they have to come to the venue.

AND DON'T FORGET THE PETS

Pets are on the rise and are the new "children" of empty nesters and busy couples. One creative casino has found a way to involve pets by creating a special dog character and Yappy Hour. Large hotels are now offering pet accommodation for guests who travel with their pets, as well as cat cafés and puppy dog retreats, where the owners and their pets are pampered.

CHAPTER 8

VIP Marketing Strategies

Using The Best Tactics To Fill Your Venue All Year Round

Mantra: Where there is one VIP guest, there are more.

DELIVERING WHAT YOU PROMISE

The biggest challenge even successful venues face is occupancy, keeping the guests visiting year round, all day, every day. In our observations, most venues are likely to experience downtimes, especially on Mondays, which tend to be slow. It is important to maximise earnings all year round.

So how do you reach out to prospective guests? Newspaper advertising has largely gone the way of the dinosaur, although a well-placed feature article about a band or an act you have scheduled, for instance, can generate guest interest, especially if you are the only venue advertising this particular show. But this kind of advertising has largely been replaced by the use of social media.

You have to talk to your prospective guests through their preferred communication media channels. In addition to email and SMS, hot social media community channels include YouTube, Twitter, Pinterest, WhatsApp, SMS, Facebook and more.

For many venue managers, using multiple, fast-changing communication channels may be a challenge, but the real challenge is in using them well. When social media was in its infancy, a smart venue manager had his assistant post an announcement on her Facebook page that a band was coming to their venue. She didn't write her post from an employee viewpoint but rather as a fan who just wanted to let her friends know about the show. The outcome was amazing: her post went viral, and tickets sold out. Voilà! Free social media works!

Making social media work for you requires having the right staffing at the right time in the marketing department to put your information out there on your guests' preferred channels. Another successful venue has leveraged its social media to engage the local community. The region is greatly affected by weather extremes and a poor road system, so the venue posts weather, bush fire and traffic alerts. The venue management are very community oriented to begin with and are known not just for their excellent venue offering but also for fund-raising efforts on behalf of charities like breast cancer research. That drives a lot more traffic to their page than would simply talking about their offers, and it really establishes them as caring, contributing members of their local community.

DOES YOUR WEBSITE DELIVER A VIP EXPERIENCE?

A regularly updated website is critical for venue success. Some venues will spend real money to build a glossy, fantastic-looking website and then simply leave it there untouched and stagnant. It is essential that all your websites and listings are kept updated and that all contact points are monitored by venue administration team members to ensure that email addresses are current and not going to a database that is not managed and that phone numbers are correct.

After we undertook a website audit, one venue known for its high standard of customer service was shocked to learn that the complaints telephone number advertised on their website was disconnected and no team member had been assigned to reply to messages sent to the email address provided by reception. This is not the right way to handle complaints. You can imagine the frustration of guests who could not get answers to their problems and retaliated with social media posts about poor customer service. This particular venue had been displaying incorrect information on its website for over six months, which caused immeasurable damage.

TOP TEN TIPS BASED ON OUR WEBSITE ANALYSIS:

1. Use font style, size and colour that is legible.
2. Make sure the address and phone number of the venue is on the landing page.
3. All email and phone contact information must be correct.
4. If using a photo on a landing page, with wording over the top, make sure the text has a still background, not one that moves or hides the words when the colours merge.
5. Make sure all website photos are clear and of good quality.
6. Make sure all links work.

7. Keep the advertised entertainment schedule and promotions up to date.

8. Update seasonal menus.

9. Be sure to respond to social media posts, especially grievances.

10. Make sure websites can be easily read on small and large mobile devices and different operating platforms.

If you are selling tickets to shows, how are your guests finding out about them, and how do they prefer to buy tickets? Many venues have gone exclusively to online ticket sales via their websites. You can undertake surveys to find out how many people are lining up for tickets, as opposed to those who call and purchase them on the phone. How many people are using the website to buy? Some venue managers believe that making guests come to the venue to purchase tickets may encourage them to stay for a while. However, a study was made of venues where long queues of frustrated guests blocked the foyer and filled the car park, and it was found that the majority of guests didn't stay but were pleased to get away from the crowds. The study also found that offering a discount for online purchases of tickets reduced long queues at the counter, kept the foyer clear for other guests and ensured the car park had spaces available.

MAKING THE MOST OF YOUR GUEST DATABASE

Back in the days before the Internet took over commerce and communication, we never used to ask for peoples' email addresses on membership or other forms. Now it's the rule rather than the exception. Once you are a member, clever venues constantly keep you up to date on specials and shows that are coming up. Using that kind of promotion to inform your membership base of community-centric events is also a great way to ensure that members will get into the habit of opening their emails rather than discarding them.

TIP

Smart venues keep email opening rates high (greater than 30%) by engaging their readers with interesting and useful information, not just a hard sell.

Venues have become smarter about asking questions on their membership forms that let them know what guests are interested in, whether it's entertainment preferences or family activities. With this information, venue managers are able to better target their advertising via their databases. Some of these venues have 50,000+ members. However, many of them do not effectively use their databases, which can be gold mines of information when utilised smartly. Databases are excellent in categorising groups of guests so that marketing can be targeted to guests of a certain age or cultural background. A targeted approach is much more effective and rewarding financially.

Social media also works well for specific electronic-type promotions and, as we have seen, can be very successful in driving guests to a new venue. One smart venue manager used social media for the opening of a new coffee shop, posting a photo of a slice of cake and a cup of coffee, with the status reading, "When you come down, show this post to our barista and you will receive a complimentary cup of coffee." As free offers go, it was small, but it went viral and was very effective.

Local advertising that depicts your venue with friendly, welcoming team members makes a promise that must be delivered. Having your guests met at the door by a Skunk with a sour face, someone who should not be on the front line, is incongruent with your venue's advertised image. If you are not what you say you are, your guests will turn around and walk back out—and there goes tens of thousands of dollars in wasted advertising. No matter how great your promotions are, don't promise more than you deliver.

WORD OF MOUTH (WOM)

The best advertising of all is positive word of mouth, and you can't buy that. You want your guests to be advocates for your venue. Ideally, your advertising or other promotions will create some excitement and get them in, but be sure that you keep them coming in by fulfilling those expectations.

One supersized venue, with a very bright, creative Director of Marketing, got a lot of great publicity for itself by applying for its own postcode. This generated free radio and newspaper publicity that was worth thousands of dollars. It became a hot media topic: why couldn't a venue the size of a small suburb in terms of its membership base have its own postcode?

The venue asked its members to write to their local government member in support of their push for their own post code. So the story lasted for a number of months. In the end, the government didn't grant them a postcode. However, the venue management went to a brewery and had a private-label beer, called Post Code, developed for the venue, and their advertisements read, "We have won. We have our own postcode!" It was a fantastic marketing campaign that engaged the members and the local community while building statewide brand recognition for their venue.

Another large Australian venue generated a lot of positive buzz for itself by linking with the Australian Government for the 2000 Sydney Olympics to build an aquatic centre that was not only the training base for the US Olympic Swim Team at the time but is now used by the community. Some other venues have looked at that partnership and are doing similar things, including talking to the local community and working in conjunction with government to give the community a facility that everybody can use, not just members of the venue.

TURNING VENUE RENOVATIONS INTO A MARKETING CAMPAIGN

Renovations can be a lengthy and messy process, but you can use it as a form of marketing, as one venue has done by advertising its twenty-one-year plan, which creates excitement and includes members in the journey. In key locations the venue has banners hanging from the ceiling, featuring photos of people who will be future guests of the venue. One banner shows a picture of two young boys saying, "We are going to represent Australia in soccer!" Another banner features a young couple who will be retired and enjoying the venue in two decade's time. It is an interesting campaign and shows that marketing doesn't always just have to be about a raffle or entertainment. It is also about involving your guests and co-creating the future together by building a venue for the future.

Advertising your upcoming or in-progress improvements can generate positive word of mouth about your venue. Otherwise, it's just months of looking at scaffolding and wondering what's going on. One smart way to make renovations appealing to guests is to offer an exclusive VIP experience to small groups by having senior managers take them on private, guided walkthroughs of your nearly finished construction. They all get to wear hard hats and go behind the scenes. Most of your guests will only see the plans you have posted, but your selected VIPs will enjoy this "backstage" look at the work in progress. Completing the visit with a beverage in the boardroom, where you show the concept plans, furnishings and finishes and ask group members for their input gets their buy-in. It all becomes real to people. They go out and tell their friends, "Oh my gosh! You should see what's behind those walls. It's really fantastic." That sort of strategy works really well to build buzz and loyalty.

Some venues advertise their renovations internally with a large LCD screen displaying a time-lapse slide show of the daily changes at the construction site. Guests see the scaffolding going up really quickly and the concrete being poured, which motivates them to go out and talk about it in their community.

One venue had a beautiful mural painted on its internal construction walls. It was like an illustration out of *Sleeping Beauty* with a vine-covered castle that looked as though it had been asleep and was awakening. Holes were cut into the mural wall at different heights, including child height, so guests could peek through and watch the progress.

RENOVATION, LAUNCHES AND OPENINGS: ENGAGING STAKEHOLDERS

"Soft openings" are a big thing, particularly in new or newly renovated food and beverage areas. A venue might have an exclusive soft opening to which VIPs will be invited and where they can enjoy a meal before the area is open to the public. This gives the chefs and the front-line team an opportunity to work together to see that everything is buzzing along, but it also, once again, gives those privileged few a reason to go out there and talk about it.

Smart managers invite community business groups to their venues for soft opening events. These groups can include real estate agents, travel agents and local businesses. Let them see your new facilities so they can get excited about using them in the future and tell others. These events also create an opportunity for the venue to highlight the materials and services that were supplied by local businesses, fostering a true community spirit. In this way, invited guests see all aspects of the venue and have the opportunity to ask questions of senior managers.

IMPROVING THE GUESTS' PHONE EXPERIENCE

What happens when a prospective guest phones your venue? Many people will make their initial contact with you via telephone to check on your location and hours or to get other information. Don't you love it when you call a venue and are forced to listen to a scratchy radio broadcast or on-hold music so boring that you hang up or, worst of all, promotions for events and holidays that have already passed? No, you don't love it, and neither do your guests. Nobody wants to hear old news. You want to know what's happening today and in the near future. Make sure that your answering system messages are pleasant, informative, up to date and easy to access.

INTERNAL MARKETING AND PROMOTIONS

Posters, banners and screen displays at various points within the venue are an excellent way to convey information to your guests. Even the humble restroom and toilet cubicle is a great space to get the attention of your "captive audience", but if the posters are torn or out of date, it's tacky and off-putting. Make sure that your custodial team members keep the posters fresh. Most venues have a lot of signage in their foyer or concierge area, but guests don't always read signs, so your team has to remember the information most likely to be asked for, the frequently asked questions (FAQ).

USING YOUR TEAM TO CROSS-PROMOTE YOUR VENUE

Another great marketing tip you shouldn't overlook concerns cross-promoting inside the venue. Team members in all areas of the venue should be confident and knowledgeable to recommend other venue facilities.

This requires team members to be well informed, proactive and outgoing. They can simply ask guests, "What are your plans for the evening?" to start a conversation and open up the possibility of the guests staying another couple of hours instead of walking out the door.

Make sure all team members know what's happening in your venue and how to share this information with guests in order to offer a VIP experience.

KNOWING THE BEST WAY TO ANSWER
FREQUENTLY ASKED QUESTIONS (FAQ)

Some venues are so large they give out little maps so guests can see the full range of venue facilities and services. Nobody enjoys the sensation of confusion and frustration that comes from being trapped in a maze, which is how guests commonly feel at venues designed specifically to "trap" guests. Todays guests are more discerning and perhaps not as easily led as guests once were.

This is where trained and knowledgeable VIP team members have the opportunity to go above and beyond in promoting facilities and services to enquiring guests.

TIP

1. Give guests little maps that feature promotions and coupons on the back of them to serve a double purpose.

2. Supply your staff with a cheat sheet that provides them with helpful suggestions they can make to guests, confirms the times when special promotions will be offered and lists useful phrases, like "Have you seen the new BMW we have as the prize for the members draw this month?", "Have you eaten in the new dining area, the pho noodles are delicious?" or "Did you know we have a great kids play area that I'm sure your children will enjoy?"

GUESTS STILL VALUE PRINTED MATERIAL

Even in the age of the Internet, printed materials are still valuable. Some venues have downsized their glossy magazine to a small, colourful booklet listing the upcoming month's entertainment and promotions and including a calendar highlighting each day's information. The calendar can be removed and placed on the fridge for all the family to see, not just venue guests who read it and misplace it.

SPONSORING LOCAL SPORTING TEAMS

It is a great idea to consider the value of sponsoring a local team when you are looking to build community relations and plant the seeds to attract prospective guests. Many venues support their local little league football club, soccer club and girls' softball team. The venue can have its name printed on the back of the players' jerseys and host the end-of-year event.

MEASURING YOUR LOCAL MARKETING EFFORTS

Often, venue managers rely on the simple concept of "bottoms on seats" to assess the effectiveness of their marketing strategies. A drop in attendance is what tells them that something isn't working. Clearly, guest surveys are a far better and more accurate tool. Surveying the broader community at local shopping centres with a ten-question survey can provide informative feedback.

SAMPLE SURVEY QUESTIONS:
1. Do you go to hospitality venues?
2. Have you been to XYZ venue (yours)?
3. Are you a member of our venue?
4. Are you a member of other venues?
5. What entertainment do you enjoy?
6. What cuisines do you prefer when dining out?
7. Does service from venue staff make a difference to your experience? How?
8. What facilities do you use when at XYZ venue?
9. What other facilities or services would you like to see offered at XYZ venue?
10. Would you attend a small focus group?

It is also helpful to regularly survey your visiting guests and members at your venue to find out which advertising is working and which promotions they like the most. Particularly with gaming promotions, surveying your players is important.

SURVEYING YOUR MEMBERS AND GUESTS USING EMAIL

Bulk email surveys to guests and members have proven to be ineffective at collecting useful information. Every day, inboxes are littered with surveys asking for your opinions, from a grocery store asking for your thoughts on its new layout to seminar organisers asking your opinion of a seminar you just attended to an agency asking you to rate the booking process and your stay on your last holiday. Your guests and members may take the time to complete your survey, but if you send out regular surveys and don't make any improvement to your venue based on the feedback, the response rate will decline. Guests and members need to see action. They get a wonderful sense of pride when they can walk through your venue and tell others, "I suggested that in the survey, and now they have it." We hear this often from focus group participants. They feel part of the business, not just guests.

THE POWER OF FOCUS GROUPS

Smart venue managers run focus groups composed of selected guests. To gain insightful feedback, the focus needs to be on the quality of the participants, not the quantity. Market research in the past has always been about quantity. However, venue managers can be given in-depth feedback when they only have four top-quality focus-group participants rather than twenty poor-quality participants, of whom more than half only sit there because they will be rewarded with a gift. How you frame your questions for the focus group is key to getting useful data. The questions need to be very narrow and specific so you are not measuring generalities. We find that following up surveys with focus groups yields very good and reliable data.

How survey questions are worded and the order in which they are asked are critical. There is no point in putting together a survey that won't provide the information you are looking for. Unfortunately, a lot of surveys are poorly written, so the time and money spent on them is wasted. A great way to recruit focus-group members is to ask for them in the guest survey.

If you are reading this line, email us for a complimentary gift: enquiries@thevipp.com.

Not everyone wants to give you personal contact information on a form, of course, but we know of one venue that found a way to make it more attractive. Management offered bar vouchers for each piece of information: if the respondents became members that night, they got $7; if respondents gave their phone number, another $2; and $2 more for sharing their email address. This is a smart way of motivating guests to give information they might otherwise be hesitant to share. One smart venue manager advertised, "SMS your email to this number for your chance to win a backstage pass to meet a celebrity." That invitation collected 250,000 email addresses and the respondents' SMS details.

Venues use this information to further target guests with text/SMS messages tailored to their interests, usually sending them out around lunchtime. It is important not to abuse this strategy, of course; nobody wants to be bombarded with messages. But if you are judicious and don't abuse the system, it is very effective.

OFFER THEM MORE

Make the most of everything your facility offers. If you have a day spa, hairdresser or shops on the premises, there are many extra opportunities you can suggest to your guests. Some venues offer a concierge service, including inviting their guests to drop off their dry cleaning. Some even post guests' letters. The venue can become a "one-stop shop". What venue managers are doing is creating the sense that once you are at the venue, you are there for the day, and they will take care of those little errands for you, freeing you up to enjoy yourself. It certainly makes guests feel like VIPs when they receive that kind of treatment. In fact, one venue with a lot of older guests advertised, "Come in and give us your prescriptions, and we will get them filled for you." It can be a simple benefit but much appreciated, especially by those older folk who are relieved to not have to go out in the heat or rain and are happy to spend the day at your venue. Make sure you let people know about all these little extras via your team and internal advertising.

When we talk to people in the hospitality industry about the ideal experience, we often hear the following from team members and leaders: "Oh, I know all about service" or "I have been serving people for years."

Of course, that's true: many of you and your team are highly experienced experts. But the fact is the attitude you bring to work with you every day is like a diamond ring you wear for years. Even the nicest stone will get dull over time if it isn't regularly cleaned and polished. We are here to help you and your team keep that diamond sparkling and bright. Your venue can be the most spectacular in the world, but all the WOW you create won't mean a thing if your guests' interactions with your front-line team and managers aren't up to the guests' expectations and don't go beyond them, consistently and continually.

EVEN A STONE CAN BE POLISHED!

Nothing stays in top form without regular and careful maintenance. Our expertise is in helping you to keep that diamond sparkling every day, for every guest who walks into your venue.

WHAT WE DO ... AND WHAT WE CAN DO FOR YOU

Our expertise and experience is with hospitality venues of all sizes and types worldwide. We work with management to get the best out of your team and help you to create the optimal guest experience.

Working with your management, we help your staff to achieve goals, analyse their values and map their self-improvement journey in order to become VIP Leaders. This includes ongoing personal coaching after completion of the programme that keeps the process on track and moving forward.

The OARS programme is our proprietary venue improvement and reporting system that can be used anywhere in the world. Trends analysis and competitor auditing are specialties that help you identify where your prospective guests currently spend their money. We not only gather the data but also analyse it via an action plan and help you to put it into practice.

Our programme offering includes our Front Line Customer Service Training that works towards perfecting your three key touch points: customer engagement, customer loyalty, and customer commitment. The Leadership Team Development Programme focusses on middle management: Team Leaders, Supervisors, Duty Managers, those you hope will take senior leadership roles. We are also active as conference speakers on the topics of customer experience, maximising the team's potential and increasing sales, based on our extensive case studies and survey data. We lead workshops and boardroom presentations, and we guide strategy development. Regular blogs, food and entertainment trends, tips and the latest in what is happening in the industry around the world can be found on our website at http://thevipp.com

We offer the following services:

TRAINING AND EDUCATION

- Keynotes and workshops at conferences and events
- Service, loyalty and sales growth presentations
- Strategic retreats and workshops

COLLECTING AND ANALYSING DATA

- Mystery Shopping, OARS programme
- Competitor audits, trends analysis
- Data analysis sessions
- Guest and staff surveys
- Focus groups

TURNING DATA INTO MEANING AND ACTIONS

- Consulting: troubleshooting, turnarounds and start-up strategies
- Business diagnostics
- Strategy development
- Executive coaching

ONGOING PEOPLE DEVELOPMENT PROGRAMMES

- Customer service training programmes

- Middle manager development programmes

- Leadership coaching

- Behavioural profiling dynamics

- Sales skills workshops

We welcome your inquiries and the chance to discuss your needs. For more information, please reach out to us on the web at www. thevipp.com. Michelle and David would love to hear from you.

THE V.I.P. JOURNEY

GLOSSARY

The VIP Journey: the Venue Improvement Programme Journey. This is a continuous effort to improve the guest experience, growth and sales results of your venue, starting from where you are now to where you want to go in the future.

The VIP Principle: focus on attracting and retaining your best guests, both current VIP guests and future VIPs.

The VIP: a guest of high value. For your department, this could be a Very Important Patron, Very Important Player, Very Important Person.

VIP culture: a display of positive team behaviours that deliver an amazing level of customer experience.

Tim Tam® moment: a moment of pure delight, a customer experience delivering above and beyond your expectations.

Tortoise-style managers: experienced managers who are organised, strategic and disciplined. They build and trust their team. They spend time on selecting team members and training and developing their team, and they use many checklists, processes and systems. They involve their team in decision making and empower their team members to take initiative

Rabbit-style managers: "run around" Rabbit Managers are disorganised, always busy and undisciplined. They love new things, especially bright shiny objectives (BSOs). With not enough time to spend on recruiting, inducting or developing systems, they are always chasing their tail. They try to do everything themselves and tend to hire and fire team members rapidly, looking for the best new one to replace the recently disengaged team member.

Puppy Dogs: team members who are willing to go above and beyond to deliver. Attributes of a Puppy Dog include willingness to please, positive attitude and high standards of personal presentation.

Skunks: team members who have a poor attitude to guests and work colleagues. Skunks' characteristics include poor presentation, a begrudging attitude and making sarcastic or negative comments that brings down others.

Sponges: People with a keen interest in continuous learning and improvement. They love personal growth, training and development. They find new things, implement new ideas and take action. "Be a Sponge."

Stones: People who express little interest or enthusiasm to learn or improve. They are not interested in personal development and are very comfortable with where they are. They loathe new ideas and avoid change. When confronted with a stone in your team, remember that even a stone can be "polished" with good management, coaching and counselling.

The Love Bucket: a metaphor for team member engagement and satisfaction. If a team member's love bucket is full, that team member is energetic and engaged. If the love bucket is empty, the team member lacks energy and engagement. You can use love language to fill up the love bucket. You can also reduce the leaks in the love bucket by removing whatever is painful and upsetting.

The Love Languages: praise, appreciation, recognition, reward, touching and you, which are a part of the time and attention a trusted and respected team member gives to another team member who may need help.

FUDGE Factors: a set of behaviours that some managers use to influence and manipulate their team members. FUDGE stands for fear, uncertainty, doubt, guilt and ego. Avoid if possible!

Sarcasm: sarcasm is the use of irony to mock or convey contempt. It is a passive-aggressive behaviour that kills teams and teamwork. As a leader, you should avoid making sarcastic comments and letting other team members make sarcastic comments. Use genuine praise and appreciation instead.

FLOW analysis: a quick look at any situation involving customer experience, based on what human brains tend to remember: primacy, recency, pain and pleasure. F stands for first impressions of the experience. L stands for last impression. O stands for "Ouch!", the pain experienced, and W stands for the WOW! factor, the most pleasurable part of the whole experience.

ROAD/BED behaviours: ROAD is a set of positive behaviours—responsibility, ownership, accountability and decisiveness—exhibited by effective leaders. BED is a set of negative behaviours that some people exhibit under stress: blame, excuses and denial. Under stressful situations, we can choose to show positive, higher-energy behaviour or resort to negative, lower-energy behaviour. This is known as playing above the line and keeping to higher energy level behaviours. Some organisations use the abbreviation DBJ (denial, blame and justify), which is similar to BED.